1.50
128

CHRISTIAN THOUGHT

CHRISTIAN THOUGHT

AN INTRODUCTION

MARIANNE FERGUSON
BUFFALO STATE COLLEGE

WAVELAND
PRESS, INC.
Prospect Heights, Illinois

For information about this book, contact:
Waveland Press, Inc.
P.O. Box 400
Prospect Heights, Illinois 60070
(847) 634-0081
www.waveland.com

Contents

Preface

I have taught the course "Introduction to Christian Thought" for twenty years and have noticed some changes in the interest of the students regarding the material. I have tried to organize the material around the recent questions raised by students. They seem more interested in topics of spirituality than in the history of the institutional churches. They want to know how to pray, so I included prayer and religious experience in the text. Students comment favorably on meditation experiences performed in class and show preference for research on Christian mystics. Therefore, I included the chapter on Christian spirituality, which may seem uncommon in textbooks about Christianity but is of interest to students.

Contemporary students seem to long for appropriate role models. They show intense interest in the person of Jesus and his relationships, with others and to his culture. I tried to contribute to their understanding of the human Jesus but at the same time explain why Christians regard him as divine.

The Bible is still a best-seller in Christian countries throughout the world. However, the variety of methods of interpretation often confuses the message. A detailed explanation of historical, critical, and literal fundamentalist interpretation is given because of the impact that these methods of interpretation have on education, society, and politics.

The academic study of Christianity offers the opportunity to examine Christianity's beginnings, development, and growth to the status of a world religion. Students are exposed to great thinkers in most of their academic subjects and should also realize the contributions that outstanding Christians have made to civilization. I included not only some outstanding Christian thinkers but also those who contributed to culture and in service to others. Contemporary students living in a pluralistic society also want to know more about their neighbors' denominations. Since they are interested in some of the denominations' beginnings and their present impact on individuals and society, I've attempted to address these topics as well.

Critical thinking is a hallmark of education, so I have tried to present major issues in Christianity with enough information to lead students to their own conclusions.

The discussion questions are deliberately provocative, designed not only to review the chapter but also to engage the students in a critical analysis of the material.

Some pedagogical aids include the definition of terms as they appear in the text, dates of major Christian events, pictures, maps, and relevant Web sites to help students understand the material. In favor of consistency, the book denotes time periods with B.C. (Before Christ) and A.D. (Anno Domini or year of our Lord).

Acknowledgements

I am most grateful for the copyediting efforts of John Weimer, an English professor at Buffalo State College. The suggestions of James Ferguson CSC, a systematic theologian, were most helpful in determining the accuracy of the material. Buffalo State College provided me with a Sabbatical, which enabled me to finish the book in a timely fashion. I extend my appreciation to Tom Curtin, Senior Editor of Waveland Press, and Associate Editors Gayle Zawilla and Jeni Ogilvie for their encouragement and support.

Chapter One

Introduction to the Study of Religion

Do you think that Americans' interest in religion has eroded in the past half century? Do you think that religion is connected to the "American Dream"? Perhaps your question may be more fundamental: What is religion and how does it affect my life?

Because of a perceived reduction in church attendance and a decrease in the number of people entering the clergy and religious life, many Americans think that religion is on the decline. One might think that secular interests such as material prosperity, increased social standing, and heightened pleasure opportunities have replaced religion as a way of securing happiness and meaning in life. Some persons look back with nostalgia to the middle of the twentieth century as the nadir of religious involvement in America. The latter third of the century has been labelled as rebellious, hedonistic, and so pleasure bent that immediate gratification became the order of the day.

However, statistical research and popular culture do not affirm the demise of religion. Concerning the changes in society over the last half century, statistics regarding belief in God, church membership, and attendance have remained very similar to those recorded fifty years ago (Gallup, 1996). In 1944, 96 percent of those polled said they believed in God. In 1996, 96 percent of those polled said they likewise believed in God. Church attendance has not changed that much over the last half of the century either. In 1950, 39 percent of those polled said that they had attended church or synagogue that week. In 1958, the number climbed to 49 percent. In 1970, the number dropped to 40 percent, but in 1995, 45 percent of those polled said that they attended church or synagogue that week. Even church membership did not seem to suffer in the past half century. In 1940, 72 percent of those polled claimed church or synagogue membership. In 1995, 65 percent of those polled reported religious affiliation with a church or synagogue.

Perhaps the greatest change occurred in the area of how much influence religion has in the lives of the people. Throughout history, religion has been the prominent shaper of beliefs and values. Communities of faith looked to their religious beliefs and practices to help make sense of their lives. The religious system bound together the community members who shared the same goals and values. In 1957, 69 percent of those polled said that religion was an increasing influence in American life. The number dropped to 14 percent in 1970, but raised to 37 percent in 1995.

One might question the accuracy of the perception of lack of religious influence in America. Evidence of religious concern for the poor is apparent in all religious organizations that house food pantries, clothes closets, dining rooms, and shelters. Most churches donate immediately to those suffering from natural disasters. Support for refugees, peace efforts, nuclear test ban treaties, and other humanitarian activities have been hallmarks of Christian churches. The number of religious publications, bookstores, Web sites, movies, and TV shows have increased in recent years. Statistics indicate that sometimes it is difficult to separate perceptions from reality. To help clarify some perceptions, we will examine the qualities of religion in general and Christianity in particular.

METHODS OF APPROACH
TO THE STUDY OF RELIGION

The two predominate approaches to the study of religion are the academic and the theological. Academic study promotes knowledge about religion, while theological study seeks to promote faith and understanding of one's own religion. The academic approach tries to be value free and objective in studying the scriptures, doctrines, practices and morality of each religion. The goal of theologians is to provide knowledge about one's own religious tradition that will lead to a greater commitment. Academic study of religion does not seek to promote faith or specific religious commitments, but rather tries to explain the beliefs and actions of communities of faith without imputing any motives. Academics try to be nonjudgmental, attempting to explain various religions from the point of view of an insider but refraining from appropriation of a religious community's faith.

When studying Christianity, it is sometimes difficult to maintain a neutral stance. One of the ways to understand a religion is through the eyes of its founder or its heroes and heroines. Limited publishing space forces one to concentrate on the contributions the founders and leaders make to religion and society. For example, Christianity was formed by its leader, Jesus of Nazareth, and Christian scholars have been honored for their portrayal of his teachings. Both academic and theological study insist upon using the tools of analytical and critical thinking when assessing beliefs and practices of various religions. For instance, although scholars have noted teachings that say women are created equal in the image and likeness of God, women are prohibited from full participation in some Christian churches. Scholars look for consistency between scriptures, doctrines, and practices of religious groups. Academics and theologians from most mainline Catholic and Protestant denominations promote a scholarly approach to the study of scripture rather than the literal interpretation advanced by Fundamentalists. Students are encouraged to form their own conclusions when academics present information, which they try to offer in an unbiased manner, while realizing at the same time that they represent an educational institution; they must be true to scholarly research.

The great diversity of Christian faith communities in the United States compels students to approach their study in the nonjudgmental stance of academics. Pluralistic societies force a student to be more objective because one cannot join all the denominations nor compare each one to one's own religious tradition. Because we are studying so many Christian groups in this book, we are using the academic approach but at the same time are trying to respect the faith commitment of its readers.

With so many varied religions in the world the question arises: Why study Christianity? Numerically Christianity is the largest of the world religions, with an estimated 1.7 billion Christians inhabiting the earth (McGrath, 1996, p. xv). Its two-thousand-year history and missionary work have extended Christianity's influence throughout the globe. It has helped to shape Western culture with its influence on art, architecture, music, philosophy, literature, and morality. Christianity continues to influence the development of science, ethics, and economic policies. The political tensions in Ireland, America, and the Balkans reflect ideals of different Christian groups.

Uses and Abuses of Religion

One of the most important contributions of religion in general and of Christianity in particular is the sense of meaning it bestows. Life must make sense to humans, and they have looked to religion to answer such fundamental questions as where we come from, why we are here, and where we are going. All religions have creation myths to explain their origins. Christians cite the Biblical creation story in Genesis to help them understand the existence and power of God. All religions try to give insight into the problem of evil. Christians see in the narrative of the Fall of Adam and Eve the part that humans played in the introduction of evil into the world. When pondering the answer to the question of where we are going, one must look to the future. Christians are not content to say that this is all there is but find hope in the resurrection of Jesus, which Paul says is the model for all the faithful.

Humans need some sense of meaning in each day of their lives that they can connect to an overarching purpose for living. It helps them overcome the response to life that is marked by randomness and insignificance. If one is loved and esteemed by God, then one sees a reason to love and esteem others. Religious rituals give meaning and continuity to life as one makes the transitional passages of birth, adolescence, marriage, sickness, and death. Christian sacraments mark these passages with appropriate rituals that connect the individual to God and each other. Religion gives solace and hope to the grieving, reassuring them that their loss will be restored in a future life. Many people find motivation and comfort from prayer, by which they can transcend this world to contact the Ultimate. Christians can reflect on scripture; on the person of Christ; and on the lives of the saints, heroes, and heroines, which can be a stimulus for meaningful meditation.

Besides needing a sense of meaning in life, humans as social beings also need a sense of belonging. Religion can offer companionship and satisfaction through belonging to a group of like-minded individuals who share their goals and values. Christianity, like other religions, can bestow a sense of identity on its followers as it defines roles and duties among the membership. Members shape their identity according to the lives of past and present heroes and heroines of their religious tradition. Thus, Christians can emulate the virtues of Jesus and the saints, whose noble deeds and sacrificial living serve as models of behavior. Outstanding figures who personify the ideals of scriptures, doctrines, practices, and group involvement act as a motivation for similar activity for others.

Humans have a need to transcend themselves and go beyond selfish concerns that can consume them. Some persons transcend themselves by talking, singing, working, and involvement with others. Others find that they have creative energies that need to be expressed. Religion provides a unique outlet for creativity in art, music, literature, media, and architecture, contributing some of the most beautiful and imaginative buildings on the earth. Christians find a vehicle for their creativity in their prayers and acknowledgement of God, who they believe transcends all creation. When admitting to a power beyond oneself, one can try to get outside of one's self and experience the joy and fulfillment that religion can give.

As any system engenders usefulness, it also sustains abuses. Religion has been blamed for wars, oppression, and prejudice against women and has been criticized for the graft and corruption of some of its leaders. Individual Christians and religious institutions have not been exempt from abuse of power. Scandals and divisions have occurred in Christianity just as in other religions. Evil resides not only in individuals but also in institutions that can abuse their power to stifle growth and creativity. Some Christians have drifted far from the teachings of Jesus but still perceive themselves as his followers. Students of religion recognize that the abuse of persons and things does not make the abused individual or object evil. For example, child abuse does not make the child evil, nor does abuse of power prevent power from being used for good. Similarly, abuse of religion does not make religion evil. Religious individuals and institutions have a history of unselfish service to others and religious beliefs can be a source of happiness and fulfillment for many persons.

SUMMARY

Popular culture has speculated on the demise of religion, yet recent statistics do not support such conclusions. Religion has maintained a positive influence, with more church-related humanitarian efforts directed to the disadvantaged and with an increase in the number of religious publications and Web sites. Religion can be studied from an academic or theological approach. The academic study promotes knowledge about religion, while theological study concerns itself with the development of faith. The academic and theological methods both stress the influence of Christianity upon culture, politics, science, and the economy.

Just as any institution and belief system have made contributions to society, Christianity has bestowed upon its followers a sense of meaning through its scriptures, sacraments, heroes and heroines, practices, and morality. It has also contributed to a sense of belonging through the community it creates, where believers can find support from other individuals who share their values.

DISCUSSION QUESTIONS

1. How can religious polls verify or challenge popular attitudes toward religion?
2. Why is church membership used as a criterion for interest in religion?
3. What is the difference between the theological and academic study of religion?
4. How does Christianity fulfill its members' need for meaning and belonging?
5. How can we say that the abuse of religion does not make religion evil?
6. How would you answer someone who claimed they believed in God, but did not need a church?

WORKS CITED

Gallup, George. *Religion in America, 1996.* Princeton, NJ: Princeton Religion Research Center, 1996.

McGrath, Alister. *An Introduction to Christianity.* Oxford: Blackwell, 1996.

Chapter Two

Sources of Information Regarding Christianity

Then, in my vision, I saw a door open in heaven and heard the same voice speaking to me, the voice like a trumpet, saying, "Come up here, I will show you what is to take place in the future." I fell into ecstasy and I saw a throne standing in heaven, and the One who was sitting on the throne looked like a diamond and a ruby. There was a rainbow encircling the throne and this looked like an emerald. . . . In front was a sea as transparent as crystal. In the middle of the throne and round about it were four living creatures, all studded with eyes in front and behind. The first living creature was like a lion, the second like a bull, the third had a human face and the fourth was like a flying eagle. Each of the four living creatures had six wings. . . . day and night they never stopped singing:

Holy, Holy, Holy
is the Lord God, the Almighty
who was, and is and is to come.

Where do think this passage originated? Do you think that it is part of scripture? If you answered in the affirmative, you would be correct—it is part of the Book of Revelation (4:1–8). The four figures have become the symbols for the four evangelists: Matthew, Mark, Luke, and John.

Christians base their beliefs upon the teachings and actions of Jesus who was Jewish and was formed by his Jewish background. Early Christians saw themselves as a movement within Judaism and used the Jewish scriptures for their prayers, beliefs, and moral guides. Christian scriptures make numerous references to Jewish history and to the Hebrew Bible, which followers of Christ call the Old Testament. A study of Judaism at the time of Christ is essential to an understanding of his heritage and the events which shaped him and early Christianity. Because scriptures are influenced by the political, social, and religious situations of the authors and their times, serious consideration must be given to Jewish conditions at the time of Jesus of Nazareth. When Christians examine the Hebrew Bible and the forces that molded it, they can better understand the New Testament.

METHODS OF SCRIPTURE INTERPRETATION

Both Christians and Jews believe that their scriptures are divinely revealed by God. The Bible, which consists of both the Old and the New Testaments for Christians, serves as a guide for living and a tool for understanding reality. Because scripture (or sacred literature, as it sometimes called) is revered by its believers as the revealed word of God, it must contain embodied truths that can be applied to life long after the scripture was written. Scripture must be interpreted because of the multiple layers of meaning that many stories contain. There are many ways to interpret scripture, but Christians usually lean toward two methods: the literal and the historical.

Literal Interpretation

Biblical Fundamentalists are those who employ a literal interpretation of the Bible. They define each word as inspired by God; therefore, each word means what it says. It is not to be nuanced or conditioned by historical situations. One of the characteristics assigned to scripture by the followers of the literal interpretation is inerrancy, which means that it contains no errors, only truth. Some literal adherents allow for mistakes in geography or science, but most allow for no contradictions within the text. Because scripture is inspired by God, who can make no mistakes, the literalist applies these words to human life today exactly as they were written thousands of years ago. For instance, if Paul said (1 Cor. 14:23) that women should not teach in church because the Jewish law forbids it, Fundamentalists would have no trouble applying the Jewish law to Christian churches. Many Pentecostal churches forbid their female members to wear pants or jewelry because the author of the letter to Timothy (1 Tim. 2:9) told "women to wear suitable clothing, without braided hair or gold or jewelry." The literalist would exclude evolution as a means of creation, because the Bible says that God created the world in six days and those days do not correspond to the pattern of evolution. Some literalists accept literary devices used by Jesus when he describes the parables. They realize that a parable does not always correspond to reality and that some figures of speech are used. When it comes to the miracles and other words and actions of Jesus, however, most literalists believe that they convey the truth exactly as they are worded.

The advantage of the literal approach is a sense of security that one experiences when resting in the revealed word of God. One perceives that the right path is being followed if one is loyal to God's word. When applying to life the truths found in the Bible, the voice of the Holy Spirit gives assurance and dispels doubt. Although one responds to the Bible in faith, this faith need not be tested. Some of the disadvantages of the literal interpretation are apparent when examining the biblical miracles in that miracles are not scientifically tested documentation, nor eyewitness accounts, nor medical or psychological records. Yet literalists accept all the miracles as happening just the way they are described in scripture. The problem of contradictions within the same gospel is not addressed. For example, in the gospel of John, chapter 3, the author has Jesus baptizing. In chapter four the words "Jesus did not baptize anyone" appear. Mark quotes Isaiah mistakenly in the beginning of his gospel and makes some geographical mistakes, but that does not interfere with literalists' claim to inerrancy.

Sometimes interpreters of scripture are divided into scholarly and nonscholarly components. Scholarly members usually produce articles or books that meet the standards of professional journals. Often scholars teach in seminaries or universities and hold advanced degrees in biblical studies. Nonscholarly members do not produce articles that appear in professional journals or in books that are reviewed by them. They do not hold advanced biblical degrees or teach in accredited universities. Many literal interpreters belong to the nonscholarly group, and their leaders function as pastors in small independent congregations, such as Pentecostal and Holiness churches. Some larger Fundamentalist congregations, such as Southern Baptists, also adhere to the literal interpretation of scripture, even though they include reputable scholars in their membership. The Southern Baptists recently passed a resolution directing women to graciously submit to their husbands as leaders in the family (Salt Lake City Conference, June 9, 1998). They base this declaration on the letter to the Ephesians (5:22), which says, "Wives, submit yourselves to your husbands as to the Lord."

Historical Interpretation

Biblical liberalism is the term attributed to those who interpret the Bible using historical-critical methods. Most mainline Protestant denominations and Roman Catholics adhere to the historical and scholarly method of interpretation. Although they attribute inspiration of God to the writings, liberals recognize them as the work of humans and therefore possibly containing errors and contradictions. They accept the cultural diversity of the writers, who used various sources and directed their writings to specific communities. For instance, Mark's gospel was written about A.D. 70 and shows the effects of the persecutions on the early Christians, who could identify with a human, suffering Jesus. John's gospel, written twenty years later to a different Christian community that was undergoing internal stress, emphasizes the divinity of Christ. The historical liberal interpreters of the Bible are not as concerned as the literalists with the miracles as proofs for the divinity of Jesus. Historical liberals see miracles as expressing the saving power of God, shown through Jesus' healing, feeding the hungry, curing the sick, and even raising the dead.

Because historical liberals accept the influence of culture on the scriptures, they will also be guided by church traditions as well as scientific and secular knowledge. Literary devices such as myths, metaphors, images, and parables are examined, so they will not be mistaken as historical facts. They employ the journalistic queries of asking who is speaking, who the audience is, why they are speaking, and where the event is taking place in order to understand the situation more fully. When examining the previous injunction in the first letter to Corinthians telling women not to teach in church, liberals would notice that it was Paul, not Jesus, who was speaking. In many situations, the audience in the synagogue could not hear the rabbi speaking because the women and children, who were in the rear and often behind a curtain, were making noise. Since they could neither see nor hear the speaker, the usual talking of mothers and children would be a disturbance to the men, who had the privileged places of standing near the speaker. Liberals would not apply this saying to the present nor forbid women to speak in church as the literalists do.

The advantage of the historical liberal method of interpretation is the honest effort to deal with the discrepancies and contradictions in the Bible. When examining the story of the possessed man from whom an evil spirit was expelled (Lk. 8:26–39) and moved into 2,000 pigs that ran into the lake and drowned, the liberal interpreters would question why swine were kept in Israel. They would likewise be critical of Jesus, who made no effort to reimburse the owners of the herd and allowed the contamination of the only water supply by rotting bodies. However, they would acknowledge that something remarkable happened—because three writers, Matthew, Mark, and Luke, give accounts of the story—but would suggest that some details were exaggerated (such as the 2,000 pigs). They would be less likely to apply to contemporary life questionable sayings of Jesus that were culturally conditioned by his times. For example, Matthew describes Jesus in bitter conflict with the Pharisees, accusing them of being hypocrites and blind guides (Mt. 23:13). By investigating the conditions in which the Bible was written, greater insight into the message and the persons can be gained.

The strong disadvantage of the historical method of interpretation is the appeal to the intellect over the appeal to faith. One must chance the possibility of rendering the scriptures equivalent to secular writings that can be dissected for various purposes. The authors might be credited with genius, but not with inspiration of the Spirit to pass on the word of God. In considering literary devices, such as metaphors, myths, images and parables, the scriptures might be reduced to pieces of interesting literature that do not require faith for their understanding.

Apocalyptic Literature

It is essential that the student of scripture understand apocalyptic literature. Apocalyptic means "to uncover" and was a most popular form of literature at the time of Christ. Whenever a society is oppressed by another group, it naturally longs for a cessation of that subjugation. Since the society members cannot express their desires openly because of fear of retaliation, they often resort to metaphors, symbols, code names, visions, and numbers to express their hope for deliverance. The Jewish society, which lived in oppression by the Greeks and Romans, had hopes that God would intervene to relieve their sufferings. The early Christians, who were suffering persecution from the Romans, had similar hopes that God would relieve them of their sufferings and punish their oppressors. Both groups believed God could directly intervene into human history or through intermediary figures to reward the faithful and punish the evil ones. The local conflict took on more cosmic dimensions by some who saw the end of this world coming soon and its replacement by a new, ideal, paradisal state that resembled the first creation before the fall of Adam and Eve. The intermediary designated by God to accomplish this feat possessed supernatural powers as God's messiah or chosen one.

The apocalyptic book of Daniel in the Old Testament, or Hebrew Bible, contains the Son of Man vision (7:13–14), which influenced the gospel portraits of Jesus.

> I saw in the night visions, and behold, with the clouds of heaven, there came one like a son of man and he came to the Ancient of Days and was presented before him. And to him was given dominion, glory and kingdom that all peoples, nations and languages should serve him; his dominion is everlasting dominion, which shall not pass away, his kingdom never destroyed.

Because Jesus sometimes referred to himself as the Son of Man, the early Christians applied this verse to him in a literal interpretation. The Jewish authors of the Old Testament did not make this application to Christ. It is important to know the apocalyptic genre of literature in order to interpret it according to the intention of the authors. When it is uncritically applied to situations not intended by the writers, mistaken interpretations can distort the message.

THE WORLD OF THE NEW TESTAMENT

Besides knowing how to interpret the scriptures, one needs a knowledge of the background of the culture and the times in which they were written. Conditions such as war, urbanization, persecution, and economic and social situations influence the authors and therefore the writings. An understanding of the conditions and culture at the time of Jesus will enable the reader to understand his message more thoroughly.

Influence of Greco-Roman Culture

Alexander the Great, when enlarging his political empire through most of the known Western world, spread Greek culture from Greece to India, encompassing the lands of Israel. He ensured the unity of his empire by installing the Greek language, literature, sports, religion, art, and architecture upon the conquered people. This process was called Hellenization after the Greek word for his homeland, Hellene or Greece. The Hellenization or Greek period lasted from about 333 B.C. to 63 B.C. Jewish reaction to Hellenization was varied; some Jews willingly accepted the sophisticated culture of the Greeks, while others objected to forced submission. When later emperors forced upon them Greek practices that were opposed to their own biblical practices, some of the Jews objected and tried to retain their traditional ways as given to them by God. A group of Jews, zealous for the law of God, even revolted in an effort to maintain their own traditional religious beliefs.

The Greek language prevailed even after the Roman occupation of Alexander's previous territory. The Romans, who defeated the Greeks, extended their empire throughout the whole Mediterranean Sea and North Africa. They called Israel by its Greek name, Palestine, after the Philistines who had once inhabited the area. The Roman emperor governed some districts, including Palestine, through a governor or procurator. The governors, assisted by the Roman army, were to keep civil order, administer justice, and collect taxes. Rome did allow the Jews some special privileges in keeping with their religious sensibilities. The Jews were not conscripted into the Roman army, did not have to offer sacrifices to the emperor as a god, and were not forced to attend court on the Sabbath. The Roman emperor appointed Herod as ethnarch, or puppet king, over Palestine. He ruled from 37 B.C. to A.D. 4. Herod won favor with the emperor by his attempts to Hellenize Palestine. He rebuilt the temple of Jerusalem with a Roman fortress at the corner, and in other non-Jewish cities he built theaters, baths, and amphitheaters, all symbols of Greek and Roman culture. After Herod's death, his kingdom was divided among his three sons, with the area of Galilee designated to Herod Antipas, referred to by the gospel writers as the killer of John the Baptist.

JEWISH BACKGROUND: BELIEFS AND PRACTICES

In spite of the foreign dominance by competing nations, the Jews were loyal to their traditions. Allegiance to only one God was central to their beliefs. Their conquerors and neighbors worshipped many gods and goddesses, but Israel's classic expression of faith is found in one of their earliest books of the Bible: "Hear O Israel, the Lord our God, the Lord is one" (Dt. 6:4).

Such respect was given to this one God, who was the Creator, that many Jews would not pronounce the name of Yahweh. Even when they wrote it, they would omit the vowels. The Israelites had a relationship with God that was defined in their covenant, or agreement. God had initiated a covenant with Abraham, in which God promised Abraham that he would become the father of a great nation and Abraham promised to obey God in return. The sign of the covenant was circumcision of male members of the community. Abraham's covenant can be dated around 1800 B.C.E., before the common era, or called by Christians B.C., before Christ.

God made another covenant with Moses that appeared to be an extension of the covenant with Abraham that is dated around 1250 B.C.E.. After traveling through the desert, Moses led the people to an area near Mount Sinai. He went up the mountain and spoke with God who gave him the law of the covenant in which is contained the Ten Commandments. The first commandment reiterated the claim to monotheism and the other commandments directed proper relations to God and each other. God promised to care for the people: "If you obey my voice and keep my covenant, you shall be my people; for all the earth is mine, and you shall be a kingdom of priests and a holy nation" (Ex. 19:5). God had entered into relationship with the chosen people and expected obedience from them as their obligation to their covenanted agreement.

The covenanted relationship has been transmitted in written form through the Hebrew Bible that Christians claim as their own, calling it the Old Testament. The first five books are considered the most sacred by the Jews because they contain the law that is to be obeyed as their part of the covenant. Christians call these five books by the Greek name of Pentateuch, but to the Jews it is the sacred Torah. Most Jews believe that the Torah was given to Moses by God for the direction of God's people. Genesis, the first book, tells the story of creation and the fall of the first parents. Exodus depicts the sufferings of the Hebrews in Egypt, God's covenant with Moses, and the Ten Commandments. Deuteronomy, the fifth book, lauds the providential care of God for the chosen people. Besides the written Torah there was an oral Torah, which, while trying to preserve the original intent, also tried to update it to changing conditions. For instance, one of the Commandments says to keep holy the Lord's Day, which to the Jews is Sabbath or Saturday. The Sabbath is kept holy by refraining from work, but the written Torah did not set time limits or the type of work that could be done. The oral Torah defined the time of the Sabbath from sunup to sundown and delineated certain work as allowable.

The book of Deuteronomy specified that Yahweh would allow sacrifices to be offered on only one location in contrast to the surrounding non-Hebrew people who performed their sacrifices to various gods and goddesses on movable sites. Solomon built a temple in Jerusalem that housed the ark of the covenant, a sacred chest containing instruments of Jewish faith. The Babylonians destroyed this temple in 587 B.C. and a smaller one was later erected. Among Herod's building projects, a restored and enlarged temple was constructed near the time of Jesus. This was the temple that Jesus visited and at which he was presented at birth. Sacrifices were offered here and devout Jews were expected to make pilgrimages to this sacred place that held the Holy of Holies, a room in which God's presence was felt. Romans destroyed the temple in A.D. 70, and it has not been rebuilt. Part of the wall has been excavated in recent years and many Jews from all over the world make pilgrimages to wail its loss. It has been referred to as the "Wailing Wall," as the lamenting voices emit that sound.

While the Jews were in exile in Babylonia, they had no temple in which to pray or offer sacrifices, yet they did not stop praising God in prayer. When they returned to Israel after the destruction of the temple, they developed houses of prayer called synagogues. The synagogue served as a gathering place for instruction where scripture was read, a sermon given, blessings bestowed, and prayers said by the congregation. Even after the temple was rebuilt by Herod, the synagogue system grew and spread throughout the areas where Jews resided. Synagogues served as gathering places for local communities of Jews who lived too far from Jerusalem to make a pilgrimage to the temple. The gospel writers portray Jesus teaching in synagogues in Nazareth and Capernaum.

Diversity within Judaism

There was some diversity within Judaism at the time of Christ.
Some of the more prominent groups were the Sadducees, Pharisees,
Essenes, and Zealots. The gospel writers (Mk. 12:18–27, Lk. 20:27–40,
Mt. 22:23–40) refer to the Sadducees as in opposition to Jesus. They
were members of the Jewish upper class, wealthy landowning aristo-
crats who were tied to the priesthood. The high priest, Caiaphas, who
arrested Jesus, came from their ranks. The Sadducees and the Pharisees dominated the Sanhedrin, the Jewish high court of religious law.
The Sadducees tried to stay on good terms with the Romans because it
was to their advantage to keep order in the country. They were most
conservative in their interpretation of scripture, limiting themselves
only to the written Torah and refusing to accept the oral additions or
clarifications. Because the first five books of the Bible did not mention
angels or the resurrection of the dead, the Sadducees rejected these
beliefs, which were prevalent at that time. The gospel writers show
them in conflict with Jesus over the issue of life after death. They
seemed to have disappeared from history after the destruction of
Jerusalem and its temple in A.D. 70.

The Pharisees did not seem to be as wealthy as the Sadducees,
nor on such good terms with Rome. They adhered to the written Torah, but they added the oral interpretations and clarifications of the
law. They were connected to the synagogue rather than the temple
and were known for their pious living in saying prayers, tithing, and
fasting. Because they accepted other writings than the first five books
of the Bible, they believed in life after death in a resurrected form, and
in angels and demons. The gospel writers show them in conflict with
Jesus over his interpretation of the oral law (Mk. 3:6), especially regarding the work to be done on the Sabbath. They survived the conflict with Rome and reorganized Judaism along Pharisaic traditions
after the destruction of Jerusalem in A.D. 70.

Since the discovery of the Dead Sea Scrolls in the caves of Qum-
ran during this century, knowledge of the Essenes has been enhanced.
Josephus and Philo, Jewish historians, and Pliny the Elder, a Roman
writer, describe their settlement near the Dead Sea.

Archeologist have uncovered a series of buildings that resemble a
monastic settlement with common rooms such as a library, dining
room, and kitchen. Small rooms off these larger rooms are presumed to
be bedrooms. Because of their small size, general thinking attributes
celibacy to the community. Large cisterns collected water which was
likely used for ritual cleansing. The Dead Sea Scrolls describe some of
the beliefs and practices of the Essenes, who lived in this desert community away from the activity of the temple at Jerusalem. Some re-

searchers believe that the Essenes hid the scrolls in the caves when they were being attacked by the Romans. Early Christianity reflects some of the beliefs of the Essenes, including the formation of a New Covenant, a ritual of a common meal consuming bread and wine, and the baptism of initiates with water. The Essenes expected the end of the world to come soon, accompanied by the arrival of two messiahs, one of priestly descent and the other of Davidic descent. Some scholars see the connection between Essene literature and the Epistle to the Hebrews, which depicts Christ as high priest and kingly messiah from the line of David.

The Zealots were a fanatical sect dedicated to Jewish religious and political freedom by ridding Israel of their dominators. They expected God to intervene on their behalf by sending a warrior king, messiah, to overthrow the Romans. They were defeated by the Romans and shared the blame for the destruction of the temple, which they refused to evacuate. Enemies of Jesus instilled suspicion of his affiliation with the Zealots when they accused him of wanting to be king of Israel.

These main factions within Israel at the time of Jesus influenced his relations with his compatriots and their perception of his role. After his resurrection, the gospel writers looked back at these groups and tried to see their connections to Jesus as messiah. The groups had varied expectations of how God would intervene in their history and how a messiah would function. The Sadducees did not expect a messiah, and the Essenes anticipated two—a kingly messiah and a priestly messiah. The Pharisees, following the prophets, expected a messiah, but not one who would suffer death at the hands of Gentiles. The Zealots expected a warrior king to lead them out of their oppression. Although their purposes and beliefs differed, they each possessed certain qualifications and performed functions that they expected messiah to fulfill.

Messianic Expectations Derived from the Old Testament

Most Jewish people, in the tradition of the Pharisees, Essenes, and Zealots, hoped for a messiah or anointed one. Messiah is a derivative of the Hebrew verb meaning "to anoint." A king or high priest was anointed for his office by the pouring of oil on his head when he was installed in office. The anointed one could be called messiah, as were Saul, David, and some other kings because they were chosen by God. Even a foreign king could be designated a messiah, as was Cyrus because God directed him to free the Hebrews from bondage in Babylonia. The word Christ is the English translation of the Greek *Christos,* which is the equivalent of the anointed one or messiah. Often Christians use the word Christ almost as a surname for Jesus.

The messiah was expected to be of the lineage of David, because of the promise given by God that the dynasty would continue forever. The Jews looked back fondly on David's and his son Solomon's reign, when Israel was at its height of wealth and power. Many Jews thought that by ridding Israel of its oppressor Rome, they would be able to restore its political status to its past glory. The Pharisees, along with most Jews, expected this resurrection of the Davidic dynasty to be accomplished by God, in contrast to some of the Essenes and Zealots, who anticipated a human revolution. Even though the kingship had disappeared from Israel because of their bondage by their enemies, the prophets kept alive the hope of a golden age when a man like David would reestablish the kingdom and rid Israel of its oppressors. The prophet Isaiah said,

> A child has been born for us, a son given to us to bear the symbol of dominion on his shoulder; and he shall be called in purpose wonderful, in battle God-like, Father for all time, Prince of Peace. Great shall the dominion be and boundless the peace bestowed on David's throne and on his kingdom to establish it and sustain it with justice and righteousness from now and for evermore.
>
> (Isa. 9:6–7)

Two forms of messiah were expected at the time of Isaiah, one a warrior king and the other a wise ruler. Since the kings were the anointed ones and the prophets indicated that the messiah would be an agent in God's purpose of reestablishing Israel, a warrior king or at least a political figure was anticipated by many. Other persons who called themselves messiahs were political figures who tried to rid Israel of its oppressors in a militaristic manner. A man named Judas and another named Simon (not Peter) led rebellions against the Romans after Jesus' death and called themselves messiahs. Other psalms of Solomon, written in the first century B.C.E., portray a righteous king who will gather together a holy people and rule without military conquests. He will be powerful in the Holy Spirit and teach his people wisdom and understanding. At no point do the prophets designate a divine being as the messiah; rather, he is to be a human agent of God.

Christians have applied to Christ the prophecies regarding an expected messiah. They claimed that he was the "prophet like Moses" described in Deuteronomy (18:15–20) whom God would raise up. There are numerous references to a suffering servant who willingly gives his life for his people in Isaiah (52, 53). Christians applied these passages to Jesus, even though Jesus did not call himself by that name. The Jews failed to accept Jesus as their messiah because he did not fit the most decisive Jewish prophesies of the messiah who would bring peace and restore Israel to its former glory. The oppression by the Romans increased after his death and ended in a disastrous war in which Jerusalem and the temple were destroyed. Jesus' death on the cross sealed the Jews' opposition to his role as messiah, because one of the most sacred books of the Torah, the book of Deuteronomy, said that a man hanged from a tree is cursed by God (Dt. 21:23). Orthodox Jews are still waiting for the messiah who will establish the kingdom of God in the manner to which their scriptures attest.

With the anticipation of the arrival of a messiah, the Jews arranged the books of the Torah in such a way that the story of their exile was at the end, leaving them to look forward to God's intervention in their history. When the Christians claimed the Hebrew Bible as their own, they felt that they could change the order of the books. They placed at the end of the bible the books of the minor prophets, which include statements that Christians think apply to Christ.

These statements leave Christians feeling hopeful, for example, consider the statement: "But you, O Bethlehem, who are little among the clans of Judah, from you shall come forth from me, one who is to be the ruler in Israel, whose origin is from old" (Micah 5:2). As another example, Christians apply to Jesus' triumphal entry into Jerusalem the quote from the minor prophet Zachariah. The readings on Palm Sunday at most Christian services include a reference to "Rejoice . . . your king comes to you; triumphant and victorious is he, humble and riding on an ass, on a colt, the foal of an ass" (Zach. 9:9). Passages in the Old Testament, which to Christians seem obviously to apply to Christ, are not that obvious to Jews.

THE NEW TESTAMENT

Christians wrote the twenty-seven books of the New Testament. The four gospels tell of Jesus' words and actions, the letters or epistles of Paul interpret the meanings of the resurrection and give suggestions for Christian living, and the Acts of the Apostles give some insights into the practices of the early church. The Book of Revelation, or Apocalypse as it is sometimes called, interprets the persecution of the early Christians, the punishments sent by God to the persecutors, and the triumph of the faithful who will reign with Christ in the future. Because the gospels tell us the most about Jesus, we will examine their content and formation.

The Gospels

The gospels are a unique genre of writing that give us the most information about Jesus the Christ. They are not biographies, because there are no dates in them, no description of the appearance of Jesus, and no character development that accompanies his childhood and teenage years. They do not fall into the category of hero tales, because there is much more material than the miracle stories. Nor do the gospels fit the genre of romances, because they are not restricted to travel, adventure, and romance. Yet some of the ingredients of biography, hero tale, and romance are included in the gospels. Perhaps the most challenging aspect of the gospels is the material that they do *not* cover. One would expect a much more complete description of the character of Jesus, his family, and his friends, as well as his ministry.

The word gospel is a translation of the Greek word *evangelion*, meaning "good news." The authors of the gospels are called evangelists, which depicts their desire to proclaim the Christian message. They tried to portray the words and actions of Jesus, whose presence they thought lived on in their midst after his death. Reflecting on the meanings of Jesus' words in his own time and interpreting them many years later in their time caused the evangelists to mix some of the words of Jesus with words reflecting later conditions. This later application of the former words and actions of Jesus contributes to the uniqueness of the genre of gospel writing.

Scholars are trying to rediscover the original words of the historical Jesus. About one hundred leading North American scripture scholars met to determine the authenticity of the words attributed to Jesus. The Jesus Seminar, they called themselves, tried to distinguish the words ascribed to Jesus from the preaching of his followers about him. Results of their study were printed in *The Five Gospels* (1993), in which the consensus of the scholars divided the words assigned to Jesus into four categories according to color. Red meant that the majority of the participants attributed the words to the historical Jesus. Pink meant that they thought that he probably said them. Gray meant that the origin of the written words was doubtful, and black indicated that the sayings definitely could not be attributed to Jesus. Although the methodology of the scholars has been attacked, the participants exemplify the serious efforts that have been made to find the original words of the man the gospel writers portray.

Religious historians try to explain the process used to write the gospels. There was a time span of forty to sixty years between the death of Jesus and the writing of the gospels. Most scholars attest to Mark's gospel as the first written around A.D. 70. If Jesus died around age 30, most of the people who had known Jesus must have died before the gospels were written. Matthew's and Luke's gospels were written between A.D. 80 and 90, and John's gospel was finished in the last decade of the first century A.D. There must have been oral traditions circulating after Jesus' death that kept his message alive before it was written down. It is likely that people in each town had memories of their encounters with Jesus. Inhabitants of Nazareth remembered his speaking in the synagogue; people from Capernaum recalled his miracles there; the population of Jerusalem could not forget the death and resurrection of Jesus. They talked about the incidents when they met and recalled the wondrous words and deeds of the man whose presence they felt lived on. Unfortunately, much is forgotten by oral traditions, and even that which is remembered often does not get written down.

Some of these oral traditions did get committed to writing because some of their fragments that together made up the finished gospels have been found. The evangelist Luke refers to these fragments, or small sections which he said he used in writing his gospel. The gospel writers collected these written fragments and incorporated them into their finished gospels. Most scholars agree to four steps in the formation of the gospels: the preaching and actions of Jesus, the oral traditions, the written fragments, and the finished gospels.

Luke described his gospel-writing process, which included these stages in the gospel tradition. The second stage consisted of eyewitnesses who knew Jesus most intimately, such as the disciples who orally passed on the message. Then a third group who were not eyewitnesses wrote down the oral accounts in fragments. Luke, who exemplifies the fourth stage, compiled his gospel from the writers of these fragments. With the advantage of hindsight, the compiler is able to evaluate the importance of persons, words, and events that he desires to record. Luke begins his gospel with a message to Theophilus, whose name literally translated means "friend of God." He described his manner of writing as similar to the way a modern writer would describe the research and writing of a term paper.

> Many have done their best to compile a narrative of the things that have occurred among us. They wrote what we have been told of those who saw these things from the beginning and proclaimed the message. An so Theophilus, because I have carefully studied all these matters from the beginning, I thought it good to write an orderly account for you.
>
> (Lk. 1:1–3).

With the material lost from the oral traditions and the time span between the life of Jesus and the writing of the gospels, it is impossible to reconstruct the life of Jesus of Nazareth according to modern standards of history. The purpose of the gospels differs from the purpose of history in that the gospels do not attempt to portray every detail of the life of Jesus chronologically or accurately. For example, Matthew and Luke designate the birthplace of Jesus as Bethlehem by placing Joseph there to register for the census. Many Christian biblical scholars think this was a construct on the part of the evangelists to fulfill the prophecies, because there is no record of a Roman census at the time of Jesus' birth.

Richard McBrien (1994), a theologian, claims their purpose is "to illustrate the eternal significance of Jesus through selected examples of his preaching, his activities, and the impact of both on his contemporaries" (p. 417). These selections were made from the stance of faith as Jesus was remembered by the community members, who believed his presence lived on after the resurrection. Approaching the words and actions from the position of faith is most apparent in Paul, who illustrates his method of receiving a tradition that he in turn passes on.

> For I handed on to you as of first importance what in turn I had received; that Christ died for our sins in accordance with the scriptures, and that he was buried and that he was raised on the third day in accordance with the scriptures, and that he appeared to Cephas and the twelve. Then he appeared to more than five hundred brothers and sisters at the same time, most of whom are still alive, some of whom have died.
>
> (1 Cor. 15:3–6)

Paul wrote this letter closer to the time of Jesus, in the middle 50s of the first century, so some eyewitnesses could have been alive and passed this tradition to him.

The gospels of Mark, Matthew, and Luke are usually called the *synoptic* gospels because they have many similar stories that stand alongside each other. Many of the stories found in Mark are also found in Matthew and Luke, although each author has his individual perspective and his own words to describe the incidents. They may have shared the same oral traditions or even some of the fragments because of the similarity of their accounts. The differences are important, because it means that they did not copy from each other. When the passages are laid side by side, the similarities are most obvious.

The frequent appearance of such parallel passages has led some scholars to assume that Luke and Matthew were acquainted with Mark's gospel. Since both Matthew and Luke contain information that they share but is not recorded in Mark, they must have had a common source, or tradition. This common source has received the name *quellae*, the Latin word for source, because scholars have not been able to locate this tradition. Both Matthew and Luke contain information that is not recorded in either of the other two synoptics, so they must have had a source unique to themselves. The diagram on page 26, known as the four-source theory, has been accepted by most recent biblical scholars as the origins of the synoptic gospels.

John's gospel seems to have some familiarity with the synoptics,

The Healing of the
Man with the Withered Hand

Matt. 12:9–14	Mark 3:1–6	Luke 6:6–11
And he went on from there and entered their synagogue. And behold, there was a man with a withered hand. And they asked him, "Is it lawful to heal on the sabbath?" so that they might accuse him.	Again he entered the synagogue, and a man was there who had a withered hand. And they watched him to see whether he would heal him on the sabbath, so that they might accuse him.	On another sabbath, when he entered the synagogue and taught, a man was there whose right hand was withered. And the scribes and the Pharisees watched him, to see whether he would heal on the sabbath, so that they might find an accusation against him. But he knew their thoughts, and he
	And he said to the man who had the withered hand, "Come here."	said to the man who had the withered hand, "Come and stand here." And he rose and stood there.
He said to them, "What man of you, if he has one sheep and it falls into a pit on the sabbath, will not lay hold of it and lift it out? Of how much more value is a man than a sheep! So it is lawful to do good on the sabbath."		And he said to them, "Which of you, having an ass or an ox that has fallen into a well, will not immediately pull him out on a sabbath day?"
	And he said to them, "Is it lawful on the sabbath to do good or to do harm, to save life or to kill?" But they were silent. And he looked around at them with anger, grieved at their hardness of heart, and	And Jesus said to them, "I ask you, is it lawful on the sabbath to do good or to to do harm, to save life or to destroy it?" And he look around on them all, and
Then he said to the man, "Stretch out your hand." And the man stretched it out, and it was restored, whole like the other. But the Pharisees went out and took counsel against him, how to destroy him.	said to the man, "Stretch out your hand." He stretched it out, and his hand was restored. The Pharisees went out, and immediately held counsel with the Herodians against him, how to destroy him.	said to him, "Stretch out your hand." And he did so, and his hand was restored. But they were filled with fury and discussed with one another what they might do to Jesus.

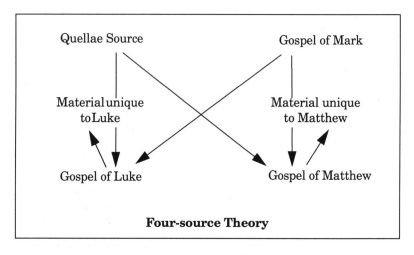

Four-source Theory

as evidenced by his rendition of the passion narratives, but most of his sources are unique to himself. As we consider each gospel, we will notice how the purposes and audiences of each evangelist influenced their selections of the remembrances of Jesus to record. Unfortunately, we do not know the identity of any of the evangelists, nor are we sure of their area of origin. None of them appear to be eyewitnesses or contemporaries of Jesus, so we cannot expect an accurate account of all his words and deeds. It is assumed that they were faithful recorders of the tradition passed on to them, so we can have some certainty about their credibility as knowledgeable judges of their material.

The Gospel of Mark. There were many problems facing the early church in the latter part of the first century. Perhaps it was some of these problems that stimulated Mark to invent a whole new kind of literature that he called gospel to deal with them. One of the problems encountered by Mark was the conquering of Jerusalem by the Romans and the destruction of the temple. It is the event of the temple disaster that helps to date Mark's gospel around A.D. 70. The temple epitomized the presence of God who cared for the Jews all through their history and its destruction caused a crisis for those Christians who were mostly ethnic Jews. The Roman persecution of Christians began with Nero around A.D. 63, and Mark's community was evidently suffering the effects. Some scholars think he was addressing Christians living in Rome. The evangelist tried to encourage his readers by showing Jesus as having great power over evil, whether it was evil spirits or storms at sea.

Mark depicts a cosmic struggle between good and evil. God had subdued the forces of chaos at creation, but at times evil powers reasserted themselves. God or God's representative must win this struggle in order to bring creation to perfect fulfillment. Mark understood the words and deeds of Jesus as the one sent by God to begin this final battle against the power of evil, and endowed by God with the power to emerge victorious. This struggle will lead to the replacement of the present age by the Kingdom of God.

The Gospel of Matthew. Although Matthew is not the first gospel written, it is usually placed first in the New Testament. Most scholars think that Matthew ties Jesus to the Old Testament by giving a list of his ancestors that take him back to Abraham, the father of the Jewish people. Matthew shows the relationship of Jesus to Moses by portraying him as a great teacher. Just as Moses gave Jews the Ten Commandments from Mount Sinai, Jesus gave the beatitudes to Christians in the Sermon on the Mount. Matthew depicts Jesus as the fulfillment of the Old Testament prophecies of the expected messiah when he repeatedly uses the formula, "All this happened in fulfillment of the scriptures." He applies to Jesus the Old Testament prophecy that said, "A young woman is with child, and she will bear a son and call him Emmanuel" (Isa. 7:14). Matthew has the angel telling Joseph not to fear to take Mary as his wife, because "The Virgin will conceive and bear a son, and he will be called Emmanuel" (Mt. 1:22).

Jesus, in Matthew, holds bitter conflicts with the Pharisees over their interpretation of the Torah. His hostility toward the Pharisees led some scholars to suspect that Matthew's own community might have met with some of this opposition. The expected return of Christ had not occurred, so Matthew gives some duties and obligations of Christians to practice until the *Parousia,* or the return of Jesus, is accomplished. Matthew is the only evangelist to use the word church, or *ecclesia,* which is translated as the group of believers. These are the faithful who will preach the Christian message to all who are willing to hear of the kingdom.

The Gospel of Luke. Although Luke builds on the tradition of Mark, he expands the information to reach a broader audience. He was an educated man, with command of the Greek language, interested in the Gentiles, and some think he might have been a companion of Paul. It is usually assumed that Luke is a Gentile, writing for Gentile Christians but with a high regard for their Jewish roots. Luke shows his universal concerns for the inclusion of all people into the kingdom by tracing Jesus' genealogy all the way back to Adam to include him as a member of the human race. Luke reminds his readers that Jesus was kin not only to Israel but to all humanity, and that his mission extended to all humankind. This inclusiveness extends to women, whom Luke designates as disciples and friends of Jesus. For almost every incident that describes

Jesus' relation to men, Luke includes one that pertains to women.

Luke employs the motif of journey to expand the Christian message. He has Jesus traveling from Galilee to Jerusalem; and then in his second book, the Acts of the Apostles, the journey extends to the known world. Luke proposes Jesus as an ethical model for all those interested in promoting the kingdom of God.

The Gospel of John. John's gospel complements the synoptics because he emphasizes the divinity of Christ while the others stress the human Jesus. Jesus appears not only as the messiah, but also in a relationship to God that designates him as equal to God. The Beloved Disciple, whom some persons think is John, is central to John's community. John addresses the problem of the failure of Jesus to return to earth during their lifetimes by identifying the Paraclete as the presence of Christ in their midst.

John's gospel is often quoted because it shows the great love of God for the disciples. Jesus speaks of the closeness of God to humans by using the image of a vine and its branches. Christians believe that the life of Christ lives in them mostly because of the teachings of John's gospel. The evangelist calls for faith from readers when he tells the disciples that they who see and believe are blessed, but more blessed will they be who do not see but still believe.

The Letters of Paul

Before the gospels were written, the letters of Paul were distributed to the early Christian communities. Paul wrote in the early fifth decade of the first century to church members at various settlements throughout the Roman Empire. Although he did not know Jesus, his experience of the risen Christ influenced his preaching of the Christian message to both Jews and Gentiles. He was a loyal Jewish Pharisee before his conversion experience, when he heard the voice of Christ. After his conversion to Christianity, Paul said that faith in Christ supersedes obedience to the Torah.

Paul developed the metaphor of the Body of Christ to express the close relationship between the faithful and Christ. He says the faithful are the body, with Christ as the head. Since humans are sinners, they need Christ to reconcile them to God. Christ's self-sacrificing death and God's exaltation of him in the resurrection forever changed humans' relationship to the Divine. Humans are expected to respond to Christ in faith if they desire to share eternal life with him. Paul's interpretation of the Christian message has affected many of the Christian teachings of today, such as justification by faith, and the mystical experience of the presence of Christ.

The Canon of Scripture

The gospels, letters of Paul and other pastoral letters, as well as the Acts of the Apostles served to bind the various Christian communities together. This earliest Christian literature encouraged faith among the communities that were separated geographically, but united spiritually. These Christian communities also were separated economically, intellectually, culturally, and socially because of the vastness of the Roman Empire over which they were spread. This kind of diversity became a challenge for Christian leaders, who espoused unity of belief and practice of the Christian message. By the second century a variety of literature had emerged along with the gospels and letters of Paul. There was some dissension among different communities who accepted some books and rejected others. Some decision had to be made regarding which books would compose the sacred canon of scripture that was recognized as authoritative and inspired by God. Some attempts to organize a sacred canon of accepted scriptures were made, but it was not until the letter of Athanasius in A.D. 367 that the twenty-seven books of the New Testament, as we know it today, were established.

SUMMARY

When looking for information about Jesus, one must consult the sources. The Jewish and Christian Bibles have yielded Christians an understanding of reality and a guide for living. Because these scriptures are considered the revealed word of God, they are often applied to life. The many layers of meaning in scriptures call for interpretation by the readers, who usually employ either the literal-fundamental or liberal-historical methods. Each approach possesses advantages and disadvantages, which must be considered when applying the scriptures to the present. Apocalyptic literature presents a challenge to contemporary readers who are not accustomed to the metaphors, codes, and images that convey its message.

It is important to understand the world from which Jesus came in order to grasp his relationship to his culture. The Jews believed in a monotheistic God whose covenanted promise to them guaranteed care for them as the chosen people. The Jews in turn agreed to obey the laws given by God and built a temple where they could offer sacrifices to the Most High. They developed synagogues as places to meet, read, and discuss scripture. The Sadducees favored the temple and the written law, or Torah. The Pharisees preferred the synagogues and the oral law. These two groups are seen by gospel writers as in conflict with Jesus. The Essenes and the Zealots contributed to the religious diversity in early Judaism and in the expectation of a messiah.

Jewish scriptures direct attention to an expected messiah, to be sent by God, who carried political and spiritual ramifications. Orthodox Jewish scholars are still awaiting the promised messiah who will come in the future. By reordering the books of the Hebrew Bible and emphasizing certain prophecies, some Christians find passages that they feel justify their claims that Jesus of Nazareth was Israel's messiah.

Early Christian writers developed a new genre of literature, called gospel or good news, to proclaim the message of the kingdom of God. The synoptic writers, Matthew, Mark, and Luke, emphasized the human Jesus, and John's gospel stressed the divinity of Christ. Gospels are not biographies or historical records and were written at least forty years after Jesus's death. Therefore they contain the interpretations of the evangelists that reflect society's conditions of their own historical times. Each of the evangelists' accounts are influenced by their purposes in writing and the audiences to whom they were directed. Paul's experience of the risen Christ influenced his letters to the early Christian communities. Because of the number of books that claimed to be authentic versions of the Christian message, the early church had to decide which ones were inspired by God. It took until A.D. 367 to determine which books would fit into the canon of sacred scripture.

DISCUSSION QUESTIONS

1. Why must scripture be interpreted?
2. Why is it important to understand apocalyptic literature?
3. How did the culture and times of Jesus affect Christians' understanding of him?
4. Why was the covenant so important to the Jews?
5. Why might Jesus disagree with the following: Sadducees, Pharisees, Essenes, Zealots?
6. Is it a good idea for Christians to apply to Jesus the Jewish prophecies of the messiah? Why or why not?
7. Why is it difficult to look at the gospels as authentic historical records of the words and deeds of Jesus of Nazareth?
8. What were the steps in the writings of the gospels?
9. Why was it necessary to establish a canon of scripture?

WORKS CITED

Gospel Parallels, A Synopsis of the First Three Gospels. Toronto: Thomas Nelson and Sons, 1967.

McBrien, Richard. *Catholicism.* San Francisco: Harper, 1994.

New Jerusalem Bible. New York: Doubleday, 1985.

Chapter Three

Jesus

T̲he gospels are the primary sources for understanding Jesus, the Christ, and they are reflections of persons who experienced Jesus in a unique way. Some evidence of his physical existence has been given to us by writers outside the Christian tradition. Tacitus, a Roman historian who lived in the first century, reported that Jesus was condemned to death by Pontius Pilate (Annals 15, 24). When the emperor Trajan asked Pliny the Younger, his lieutenant in Syria, to report on the actions of the Christians in his territory, he said that they worshipped Christ as a God and took an oath not to hurt anyone (Antiquities Epistola, 18, 63–64). Josephus, a Jewish historian, referred to James as the brother of Jesus who is called the Christ (Antiquities, 20, 200). In his *Antiquities of the Jews* (trans. Feldman, 1927), Josephus is quite specific about the person and activities of Jesus.

> About this time [during the term of Pontius Pilate, Roman governor of Judea, 26–36 C.E.], there lived Jesus, a wise man, if indeed one ought to call him a man. For he was one who wrought surprising feats, and was a teacher of such people as accept truth gladly. He won over many of the Jews and many of the Greeks. He was the messiah. When Pilate upon hearing him accused by men of highest standing among us, condemned him to be crucified, those who had in the first place come to love him did not give up their affection for him. On the third day he appeared to them restored to life, for the prophets of God had prophesied these and countless other marvelous things about him. And this tribe of Christians, so called after him, has still to this day not disappeared. (18, 63–64)

There is some concern about the authenticity of Josephus' words in that some sentences appear to be inserted, perhaps by Christians. Howard Kee (1998), a historian of religion, says, "L. H. Feldman, an eminent Jewish scholar who edited and translated this document, thinks, however, that 'He was the Messiah' are the only words added by Christians" (p. 19). Josephus might not be giving his own opinion regarding the rest of the words but merely repeating the claims made by Christians about Jesus. It is important to cite outside authorities who lived close to the time of Jesus in order to verify his historical existence. Jesus is regarded by Christians and non-Christians alike as a real human being who lived in a geographical place that still exists. The towns and regions mentioned in the gospels still remain today much the same as in his time.

THE LIFE OF JESUS

Was Jesus born on Christmas? Scholars do not agree on the exact date of the birth of Jesus. They usually agree that he was born sometime between 0 and A.D. 4. The date of December 25 was not decided upon until the fourth century. Two of the gospel writers note the birth of Jesus. Matthew tells the story through the eyes of Joseph (who was betrothed to Mary) and Luke through the reflections of Mary. The stories have been referred to as the infancy narratives because they portray the conception and birth of Jesus. Matthew reports of the confusion of Joseph, who discovers that Mary is pregnant before they had any relations together. Joseph, who is a descendant of King David, is told in a dream that he should take Mary as his wife because the child was conceived through the power of the Holy Spirit. Matthew sees the conception as fulfilling the scriptures: "The virgin shall conceive and bear a son, and he shall be called Emmanuel" (Mt. 1:22–23). He is referring to a prophecy given to a Jewish king (Isa. 7:14), which Matthew, in post-resurrection faith, interprets the Hebrew Bible to apply to Mary. Luke has the angel speaking to Mary and telling her that she has found favor with God and will bear a child to be called Jesus, or Emmanuel. Mary questions how this can happen because she is a virgin. The angel tells her that she will conceive by the power of the Holy Spirit, and that the child will be a descendant of David and his kingdom will have no end (See Lk. 1:28–33).

The accounts differ again when describing the actual birth of Jesus. Matthew has the new family living in a house in Bethlehem where they are visited by Magi, who bring gifts from the East. King Herod wants to kill the child because he fears a rival, but Joseph is warned in a dream to take the child and his mother to Egypt in order to escape the murder. Luke has Mary and Joseph leaving Nazareth to be enrolled in a census in Bethlehem, Joseph's city. They can find no place to stay and find shelter in an animal stable, where the baby is born. Lowly shepherds, who traditionally have been regarded as socially inferior by Jewish society, come to pay homage to the child. Luke has the family partaking of the Jewish ritual of circumcision and the presentation of Jesus in the temple where he is hailed by Anna the prophetess and Simeon the holy man.

Although the accounts diverge, both stress some important theological points. Both accent the virginity of Mary, and Jesus as her firstborn. Joseph is never described as the father of Jesus, but Mary, in these and other passages, is referred to as the mother of Jesus. Jesus is born in the town of Bethlehem, which is King David's city and an appropriate birthplace for his descendant. The name of Jesus is given by God, not by Mary or Joseph, indicating the power associated with naming. The genealogy of Jesus given by Matthew traces his ancestors back to Abraham and by Luke's genealogy to Adam, both emphasizing that Jesus is a member of the human race. Although the accounts may differ in details, the humanity of Jesus is stressed by both evangelists. Jesus grows up in Nazareth according to both authors, who tell very little of his childhood.

The adult Jesus began his public life near the Jordan River, where he was baptized by John the Baptist. He gathered around him a small group of disciples who came from the area of Galilee. They traveled together as Jesus began to teach about the kingdom of God. His preaching was accompanied by healings, which attracted a large audience clamoring to hear the itinerant preacher. Although Jesus was called rabbi, he did not confine his teachings to the synagogue but preached in open fields, on boats, and on mountainsides. He likewise deviated from the traditional role of the rabbi in that he seldom appealed to the authority of the Torah, nor did he found a school.

Mark refers to Jesus' occupation as that of carpenter. John Meier (1991), a scripture scholar, translates the Greek word *tekton* as woodworker because he thinks that "it can be applied to any worker who plied his trade with hard material. . . such as wood, stone or ivory" (p. 281). Since houses in Nazareth were made mainly from stone, wood would have been used for doors, beams, locks, furniture, plows, and yokes. Although the economics of the American middle class would not adequately reflect the situation of the middle-class group to which Jesus belonged as a tradesman, he was not considered poor. He easily could have obtained an education that included a knowledge of scripture that was standard for young men of his class at that time. Meier claims that "as the firstborn son, Jesus would have been the object of Joseph's special attention, both in training him for a trade and in seeing to his religious education" (p. 350). Dominic Crosson (1994), another scripture scholar, says that Jesus, as an artisan, belonged to the 5 percent of the population that was lower in social status than the peasants. He says, "Since 95 to 97 percent of the Jewish state was illiterate at the time of Jesus, it must be presumed that Jesus was also illiterate" (p. 25). Crosson admits that in an oral culture such as Israel,

"The foundational narratives, basic stories, and general expectations would be known by most Jews" (p. 26). These two divergent opinions reveal the variety of thoughts regarding the historical Jesus. But they both show the difficulty of attaining certainty regarding events and words of a man who lived over 2,000 years ago.

TEACHINGS ON THE KINGDOM OF GOD

John's gospel portrays Jesus' ministry as lasting about three years, while the synoptics refer to only one passover indicating a possible one-year ministry. Central to his preaching was the kingdom of God, a term familiar to Jesus, because the Old Testament or Hebrew Bible refers to God as King (Dt. 33:5). Later apocalyptic writings such as Daniel 7:13–20 refer to a universal kingdom that will come in the future. The kingdom of God is also referred to by present-day Christians as the kingdom of heaven and also the reign of God, a term some Christians prefer because it lacks spatial restrictions.

The concept of the kingdom has two distinct dimensions. Some Christians favor the kingdom as a future one that lies beyond time and space. Others look at it as the totality of God's activity in creating the world and God's present involvement on behalf of the covenanted people. Some people who emphasize the future aspect of the kingdom see it as a reward in the next life for their good deeds on earth, and they look forward to a happy life in heaven in union with God. Many who would stress the coming of the kingdom in this world would notice a huge discrepancy between what ought to be and what is in human society. The present state is marked by injustice, hunger, death, anguish, lack of freedom, and sin. Eamon Bredin (1986), a theologian, says, "So if God's reign is to be effective,. . . it will involve overcoming all injustice and the establishment of God's own justice. . . . of help and protection for the helpless, the weak and the poor" (p. 78). Jesus spoke of the kingdom as coming in the future and also as being here in the present. References to a future kingdom appear in Lk. 13:29, where Jesus compares heaven to a future banquet, and in Mk. 14:25, where he tells his disciples that he will not eat nor drink with them again until he drinks the new wine in the kingdom of God. He taught the prayer known as the "Lord's Prayer" or the "Our Father," asking for God's kingdom to come. Jesus also relates to parables that say a final sorting out will occur before the kingdom is attained. In the parable of the net (Mt. 13:44), he says that after the fishermen divide their catch, they sort out the bad fish from the good and throw away the bad fish.

Jesus makes reference to the kingdom as being here all around us. "The time is fulfilled, and the kingdom of God has come near" (Mk. 1:15). "The kingdom of God is not coming with things that can be observed; nor will they say, 'Look, there it is' or 'there it is,' for the kingdom of God is among us" (Lk. 17:20). Jesus makes the kingdom seem most immanent in Mk. 9:1 when he says, "Some are standing here who will not taste death before they see the kingdom of God come with power." When examining the words of Jesus, there appears to be some tension between believers in the vision of the kingdom arriving in the present and those who believe its coming will be in the future. But a closer examination indicates that the kingdom could begin in time and continue into the future. By emphasizing both dimensions of the kingdom—present and future—Christians might determine more fully the basic teachings of Jesus.

If Christians restrict their vision of the kingdom as a future life with God in heaven, there is a danger that they might ignore the plight of their neighbor while concentrating on personal salvation. It is questionable to reduce one's vision of the kingdom only to the future because the present will then become a meaningless waiting period. American slaves were told that if they would only suffer their injustices now, they "would have pie in the sky in the great bye and bye." Sole emphasis on the future kingdom justifies Marxist claims of religion as the "opium of the people" because it desensitizes them to present injustices and inequalities. On the other hand, concentration on only the kingdom of this world could cause Christians to become activists for the cause of others in a humanitarian sense and to ignore the motivation behind these actions as rooted in love of God. If the kingdom is limited only to the present, Christians might suffer the delusion that by simply improving conditions in society, they will be responsible for bringing about the kingdom here and now. The parables of Jesus emphasize the presence or reign of God in both the present and the future. The New Testament writers indicate that the kingdom is made real in some way in the present, but the fullness of God's reign is projected to the future.

Jesus' Preference for the Poor, Outcasts, and Women.

One of the obstacles to Jesus' teaching about the kingdom coming in the present was the purity system of the Jewish law. It set up boundaries between persons, places, times, things, and even social groups. Because holiness was perceived as separation from everything that was considered unclean or impure, the purity system established strong polarities between the acceptable and nonacceptable. One could be born impure by being Gentile, lame, blind, deaf, a leper, chronically ill, or by having any other physical deformity. The poor were sometimes considered impure because they did not have the economic ability to observe all the purity laws, such as paying temple tithes. Bodily fluids, especially blood that was connected to women's menstrual cycle, were considered impure. Because the birth fluids were tainted, a purification ritual was prescribed for new mothers. Some occupations did not meet the purity code. For example, tax collectors were considered outcasts because they did not engage in acceptable livelihoods.

The purity system created sharp social boundaries between the pure and impure, Jew and Gentile, rich and poor, men and women, and the physically whole and those who were not whole. Jesus constantly crossed these boundaries in his preaching and actions. He healed the blind, the deaf, and the lame. He preached to the poor and befriended tax collectors and women. He made an outsider the hero of the Good Samaritan story. By sharing meals with such people, Jesus violated the purity rules surrounding food. In the Jewish world, sharing a meal had a strong social significance because it implied mutual acceptance. Jesus was accused of eating with tax collectors and sinners and of being a glutton and a drunkard because of his eating preferences. He did not limit himself to those on society's fringes but included among his acquaintances people of accepted respectability and stature, such as Nicodemus and Joseph of Arimathea. His inclusiveness of all persons, regardless of the purity laws, established him as a friend to some and an enigma to others.

Jesus seemed to prefer the poor in that he preached the good news to them. He mentioned them first in his beatitudes, when he said, "blessed are you poor" (Lk. 6:20). He was a tradesman, not an aristocrat or member of the priestly class. He performed most of his miracles for the poor and dependent, such as raising to life the son of the widow of Naim. He commended the poor widow who put all that she had in the temple collection box and denigrated those wealthy who gave out of their plenitude. The poor publican who humbly admitted his sin was exalted by Jesus at the same time that he demeaned the rich Pharisee.

Norman Perrin (1967), a scripture scholar, claims that "Jesus' acceptance of outcasts was the primary source of the hostility that his ministry generated. It was an extraordinary action for a religious figure in the Jewish tradition" (p. 107). Some of the outcasts would include tax collectors because, although they were well off, they made their money by cheating the people and collaborating with the Gentiles.

Jesus befriended Zaccheus, a known tax collector (Lk. 19:3), and even invited himself to eat at his house. Matthew, a former tax collector (Mt. 10:3), became a disciple of Jesus. Jesus commended the unnamed woman, whom Luke (7:37) calls a sinner, when she washed his feet with her tears and wiped them with her loose hair which by custom should have been bound. Jesus approached an often-married Samaritan woman, who was an outsider, and entered into conversation with her (4:8).

Perhaps the worst outcasts of all were the lepers. Their disease had marked them for death, and therefore they were not only unclean but also untouchable. They were cast out from their towns and villages because of their disease and could only regain entrance if their priests declared them cured. Jesus showed his respect for the law when, after curing a man with a dreaded skin disease, he told him to show himself to the priest so he could regain entry to the community (Mk. 2:44).

Jesus showed regard for everyone, including women. According to Jewish law, women did not have the rights and privileges of men in that they had to engage in arranged marriages that they could not terminate. Only the husband could initiate divorce. Men and women were not to engage in conversation with each other in public. A woman was dependent upon a man all her life—either her father, her husband, or her son. She was not allowed to read the Torah, as it warned that woes should be expected to the father that teaches his daughter the Torah. During her menses, she was not allowed to go out of the house, to touch a man, or even to prepare his food. Women could not go beyond the lower court of women in the temple, could not belong to the priesthood, and had to defer to men in the synagogue.

Jesus, in contrast, treated women with respect and dignity. He spoke to them in public, allowed them to learn as disciples did, and even numbered them among his followers. Perhaps the most remarkable treatment of women is their call to discipleship. Jesus frequented the home of Martha and Mary, who were sisters. John's gospel indicates that Lazarus was their brother.

> As Jesus and his disciples went on their way, he came to a village where a woman named Martha welcomed him into her home. She had a sister named Mary, who sat down at the feet of the Lord and listened to his teaching. Martha was upset over all the work she had to do, so she came to him and said, "Lord, do you not care that my sister has left me to do all the work by myself? Tell her to come and help me." The Lord answered her, "Martha, Martha, you are worried and troubled over many things, but only one is needed. Mary has chosen the right thing and it will not be taken from her."
>
> (Lk. 10:38–42)

Jesus defends Mary because she has dared to step out of the role destined for women, that of homemaker. She has taken the role of disciple by sitting at Jesus' feet and listening to him. When Martha wants Jesus to make Mary conform to society's accepted role, Jesus calls her by name twice, "Martha, Martha." Calling someone twice in scripture denotes a close relationship between that person and God. For example, God called "Samuel, Samuel" (1 Sam. 3:4), and Jesus called "Simon, Simon" (Lk. 22:31). Jesus and Martha must have had a close relationship that resulted from numerous visits by Jesus to her house. Luke's gospel stresses the kingdom of God, with the Martha and Mary story located in the center focal point of the gospel. The passage about Jesus teaching the "Our Father" prayer immediately precedes it, and the Good Samaritan story follows it. These stories illustrate two ways to reach the kingdom, one though prayer and learning and the other through service. Mary exemplifies discipleship, and Martha exemplifies service. Both women together model the ideal follower of Christ, who both prays and serves.

Jesus also chose women to be preachers. The Samaritan woman followed Jesus' command to "go and tell" her people about Jesus fulfilling the role of Messiah (Jn. 4:28). Her preaching brought amazing results because her townspeople came to hear him. Women are the first to witness the empty tomb and they, too, "go and tell" the marvelous news (Lk. 24:9). Mary Magdalene is the first to see the risen Christ (Jn. 20:18), and she witnesses to it by telling the apostles. Jesus allowed women to travel with him.

> Sometime later Jesus traveled throughout the towns and villages, preaching the good news about the kingdom of God. The twelve disciples went with him, and so did some women who had been healed of evil spirits and diseases: Mary (who was called Magdalene), from whom seven demons had been driven out, Joanna, whose husband Chuza was an officer in Herod's court, and Susanna, and many other women who used their own resources to help Jesus and his disciples.
>
> (Lk. 8:1–3).

It would seem that Jesus' mission of preaching the kingdom was carried on by both his apostles and disciples, which included men and women.

Parables

Jesus taught often by the means of parables, which were short discourses that made comparisons. He used parables to explain the kingdom of God, comparing it to a pearl of great price (Mt. 13:45) or a treasure in a field (Mt. 13:44). When he compares the kingdom to a wedding banquet (Mt. 22:8), one notices that the invited guests did not come, so the invitation was extended to the poor. Sometimes parables provide moral instruction, but the moral choice is left to the listener. Jesus' parables were sometimes paradoxical in that they upset conventional thinking and challenged new ways of reflecting upon situations. The parable of the prodigal son (Lk. 15:11) showed the unconditional love of the forgiving father, which could be compared to the goodness of God.

The parables focus on human life and how humans relate to each other. Pheme Perkins (1981), a scripture scholar, says, "This dimension of the parables makes them applicable to every person, not just to first century Jewish merchants, farmers and the like" (p. 4). The Good Samaritan parable (Lk. 10:25) challenges the individual to compassionate service to the unfortunate. The parable of the rich fool (Lk. 12:13) forces one to evaluate one's attitude toward material goods. The vineyard parable (Mt. 20:1), where those who only worked the last hour received the same amount of wages as those who toiled all day, causes one to examine one's attitude toward jealousy, prejudice, and justice. The timelessness of Jesus' parables apply today as they continue to inspire Christians to reflect upon their values, attitudes, and goals.

Miracles

Jesus did not only speak but also gave credence to his words by his deeds. The gospel writers do not use the term "miracle" but rather "signs," "wonders," "works," or "works of power." Christianity has always accepted the fact that Jesus performed miracles as signs of revelation of the power of God. From the scientific point of view, it is difficult to define what constitutes a miracle, because miracles appear to upset the laws of nature. Miracles in New Testament times were not understood as something contrary to natural law, but as something that rouses admiration. Miracles seem to support the preaching of Jesus as he heals the lame, feeds the hungry, and even raises the dead to life. When John the Baptist's disciples asked Jesus if he was the one who was promised, he answered, "The blind see, the lame walk, the lepers are cleansed, the deaf hear, the dead are raised and the poor have the gospel preached to them" (Lk. 7:22).

The ancient Jews believed that God not only created the world, but God intervened in important events such as the exodus event and the phenomena that accompanied it, including the parting of the waters and the sending of manna. Miracle workers, particularly healers and exorcists, were accepted in Judaism in the time of Jesus. Sometimes sickness was attributed to devils, especially if sickness appeared psychological and thus difficult to understand. Religious historian Howard Kee (1986) claims that the miracles are central to the gospel tradition and therefore must be related to historical fact. He says, "About one fifth of the literary units in the synoptics allude to miracles of healings and exorcism, and a large portion of the Johannine gospel is concerned with miraculous signs" (p. 86).

However, not all theologians are ready to accept every miracle as being historical. There are some serious questions about the nature of miracles, such as Jesus walking on the water (Mk. 7:9) or the calming of the storm on Lake Galilee (Mk. 4:41). They concede that there might have been an actual storm but that some of the details have been heightened. Jesus did not use the miracles as proof of divinity because he never referred to himself as divine. Humans in the Old Testament such as Elijah and Elisha performed miracles, as did the disciples of Jesus before and after his death. He never used his miracles for personal gain and seemed to prefer the poor, sick, women, and other oppressed persons as recipients of his works. He did show concern for some people of faith from the higher social classes. He raised to life the daughter of Jairus (Lk. 8:41) and healed the Roman officer's servant (Lk. 7:10). The gospel writers depict Jesus' miracles as pointing to the reign of God, in which the powers of evil will be overcome and the powers of good will prevail.

ETHICS OF JESUS

Sometimes the ethics of Jesus have been called radical because the word radical comes from the Latin word *radix,* which means root. If one goes to the root of things, one must examine the essentials, or the root idea, behind one's actions. Jesus stressed the inner attitudes of persons that motivated action. In ancient times morality was determined by the law of vengeance. If someone knocked out your tooth, you were allowed not only to remove the other person's tooth, but also could gouge out an eye. If someone raped your sister, then you were entitled to kill his sister. Hammurabi's code of laws appeared more just, because he said that you could only have "a tooth for a tooth and an eye for an eye." Moses' Ten Commandments did not mention vengeance or justice but told the Israelites to refrain from any mistreatment of others.

Jesus went beyond the overt actions of Moses to the inner attitude that provokes the actions. In his Sermon on the Mount (Mt. 5:1–11), he commends those who are poor in spirit, those who are humble, those whose greatest desire is to follow God's will, the peaceful, the pure in heart, and the merciful. Jesus reminds them that in the past they were told not to commit murder, but now he tells them to refrain from anger. They were told before not to commit adultery, but Jesus takes it further and tells them not to look at a woman with lust in their hearts. He tells his hearers not to take revenge on those who hurt them but to love their enemies.

Jesus' teaching on forgiveness was perhaps the most radical of his approaches to ethical behavior. In answering Peter, who wanted to show how magnanimous he was by offering to forgive his brother who sinned against him seven times, Jesus told him to forgive "seventy times seven times" (Mt. 18:22). One of the petitions in the prayer that Jesus taught, called the "Our Father," is asking God for forgiveness. There is a condition placed upon that request that says, "Forgive us our trespasses as we forgive those who trespass against us" (Mt. 6:12). It appears that forgiveness by God is contingent upon the petitioner's ability to forgive others. Jesus' teaching on forgiveness showed a marked departure from the law of vengeance or the justice of Hammarabi. Jesus went beyond the legalism of his day when he saw a human in need. He cured people on the Sabbath day, which was designated as a time when no one should work. Even when his enemies deliberately set up a man with a withered hand on the Sabbath to see if Jesus would break the law in order to cure him, Jesus put the good of the human before the law and made him whole (Mk. 3:1). He told his disciples that his commandment was to "Love one another as I have loved you. The greatest love a person can have for his friends is to give his life for them" (Jn. 15:12).

PASSION AND DEATH

Jesus' teachings and actions provoked hostility from the religious and political authorities. His teachings on the kingdom seemed dangerous to the Romans, who had executed other insurgents. He stirred up suspicion when the admiring crowds followed him. His cleansing of the temple would not have gone unnoticed by Pilate. The sign on the cross suggests that he was executed as a messianic pretender, "King of the Jews." Albert Nolan (1992), a theologian, connects the death of Jesus to the kingdom:

> In these circumstances death was the only way of continuing to serve humankind, the only way of speaking to the world, the only way of witnessing the kingdom. Deeds speak louder than words, but death speaks louder than deeds. Jesus died so that the kingdom might come. (p. 141)

Jesus had firsthand knowledge of the fate of those who would challenge the religious or political authorities. He had seen crucifixions and stonings and knew the pain they inflicted and horror they instilled. In the tradition of his many shared fellowship meals, he called his friends together for a supper. Jesus is pictured by the synoptics as adding an important feature to the standard Jewish group meal of bread and wine. He linked the symbolism of the shared bread and wine to his impending death by saying that he would not eat or drink again until he did so in the kingdom (Mk. 14:25).

After the supper, Jesus and his disciples walked to the Garden of Olives to pray and await his arrest. The humanity of Jesus became most apparent as Mark reported that he recoiled in terror and fear at the prospect of pain, suffering, and death. Jesus said, "The sorrow in my heart is so great that it almost crushes me" (Mk. 14:32). He did not hold to his own desires but willingly acquiesced to what he thought was God's will for him by saying, "Not my will but yours be done" (Mk. 14:36). Then, with courageous resolve, he left the garden to meet his betrayer.

Pontius Pilate condemned him to a death that was usually reserved for traitors, slaves, criminals, and political insurgents. Roman custom called for a flogging before the execution, which often left the victim weakened and in great pain. Two soldiers on either side of the stripped victim struck him with leather thongs, to which pieces of stone and sharp bones had been attached. These tore at the flesh until many of the victims passed out in pain. Jesus was too weak as a result of the beating to carry his cross by himself, so Simon of Cyrene was recruited to help him carry it to the spot of crucifixion. Tradition says it occurred on a small hill called Golgotha, where Jesus was nailed to a cross and hung for three hours in humiliation and pain until his death. Besides the physical suffering, Jesus experienced the psychological suffering of abandonment. His disciples ran away, the crowds that he had once helped ignored him, his enemies mocked him, the soldiers took his clothes, and he wondered if even God had forgotten him. Mark reports that one of his utterances from the cross was, "My God, my God, why have you forsaken me?", which is the first line of a Jewish psalm (Mk. 15:34). The evangelists portray the desolation of the situation by describing the darkness that had fallen over all the earth. Jesus' dead body was placed in the borrowed tomb of Joseph of Arimathea that was hewn from rock. A large stone was rolled across the entrance and a seal put upon it that would show any evidence of tampering.

THE RESURRECTION

Each of the gospel writers gives us an account of the empty tomb. Gerard Sloyan (1983), a theologian, says, "It is impossible to understand the resurrection if we think of it as the resuscitation of a dead man" (p. 146). Jesus did not come back to life in the manner that Lazarus did, because a temporary return to life would necessitate a death all over again. Jesus did not return to ordinary life but entered a most profound transformation. He was encountered in a new way by the disciples who did not always recognize him at first (Lk. 24:30). Some of the Jewish beliefs at the time included belief of an afterlife. The Hebrew Bible tells of Elijah (2 Kings 2:1) and Enoch (Gen. 5:34) being lifted up to heaven, and the psalmists spoke of union with God after death (Ps. 13a). One of the Maccabean sons, who was being tortured and about to be killed, said to the king, "You accursed fiend, you are depriving us of our present life, but the King of the world will raise us up to live again forever" (Mac. 7:9). The Jewish teachings on life after death included faith in a God who would save them and extend his justice to the afterlife.

It is difficult to determine precise historical reconstruction of the earliest Easter events because the gospel narratives underwent a period of development. The first account comes from Paul.

> I passed on to you what I received which is of the greatest importance: that Christ died for our sins and that he was raised to life three days later, as written in the scriptures; that he appeared to Peter and then to all the apostles. Then he appeared to more than five hundred of his followers at once, most of whom are still alive, although some have died. Then he appeared to James and then to all the apostles. Last of all he appeared to me.

> (1 Cor. 15:3–8)

Paul goes on to say that because Christ was raised from the dead, so will his followers. "The truth is that Christ has been raised from the dead, as the guarantee that those who sleep in death will also be raised" (1 Cor. 15:20).

The evangelists refer to an empty tomb and to appearances by Jesus to his followers. A great change occurs over his followers, who no longer remain in hiding because they fear that the same fate dealt to Jesus will befall them. Rather, they courageously begin to preach that the same Jesus who had been crucified has risen from the dead and now sits at the right hand of the Father in heaven. Matthew said that in one of Jesus' appearances to the disciples "they worshipped him," indicating that they were treating him as divine (Mt. 28:16). The passion story, with its disastrous outcome of the failure of the proclaimer of the message of the kingdom of God, now endures because his followers believed that God had raised His Son to glory.

There are some difficulties regarding the gospel stories of the resurrection because of the discrepancies in the accounts. Although each evangelist gives the time as early Sunday morning, the names of the women who find the empty tomb are different (Mt. 28:1; Mk. 16:1, Lk. 24:10). Another difficulty involves the vested interest of the reporters. The gospel accounts are not the unbiased reports of disinterested observers but persons who would profit by this astounding event. If it were not for the resurrection, the whole movement might have died. On the other hand, the resurrection seems to have been totally unexpected by Jesus' followers. The behavior of the disciples, who all ran away and hid behind locked doors, did not indicate any foreknowledge of the event. The disciples did not immediately recognize Jesus when he appeared to them after the resurrection. Mary Magdalene thought he was the gardener (Jn. 20:16), and the couple on the way to Emmaeus did not recognize him until the breaking of the bread (Lk. 24:30).

Perhaps the greatest obstacle to the historicity of the resurrection is the lack of direct evidence given by eyewitnesses. The resurrection is not described because there is no one who claims to have witnessed the event. However, the very fact that the gospel writers do not tell the story, embellished with wondrous fanfare and cosmic developments, could give the stories more credibility. It was common at the time to venerate the tombs of prophets and other outstanding men such as King David, whose tomb became a place of pilgrimage by the Jews even until today. Yet Alister McGrath (1997) notes the lack of veneration at the grave of Jesus:

> But there is no record whatsoever of any such veneration of the tomb of Jesus by his disciples. This would have been unthinkable unless there was a very good reason for it. That reason seems to be the simple fact that Jesus' body was absent from the tomb. (p. 103)

The narration of the appearances of Jesus after the resurrection have also undergone some development. Luke is careful to say that he was not a ghost because he had flesh and bones and ate and spoke with the disciples (Lk. 24:39). John has him showing his wounds, which provoked Thomas's wondrous reply, "My Lord and My God" (Jn. 21:28). Jesus seemed to be able to transcend space, as he entered the room where the apostles were hiding without going through the locked doors. He also seemed to be able to transcend time, because he told Mary Magdalene not to cling to him because he had not yet returned to the Father. He told her to tell the disciples that "I am returning to him who is my Father and their Father, my God and their God" (Jn. 20:17).

The disciples' belief in the resurrection caused them to view Jesus differently. They perceived Jesus as raised to a new level of existence beyond time and space, and they ascribed to him the titles of messiah, Son of God, Lord, and Savior. Their resurrection faith enabled them to look back on their memories of Jesus of Nazareth, on his words and deeds, and to understand them as fulfillment of prophecies of their Hebrew faith. The believers then could apply to Jesus the titles, worship, and devotion that they had reserved for God alone. The Jewish disciples remembered the only scriptures they knew, the Hebrew Bible, in order to come to some understanding of the ignominious death that befell their friend and leader. They looked at God's promise to David through the prophet Nathan, "Your house and your kingdom shall be made sure forever before me, your throne shall be established forever (2 Sam. 7:12). The Jewish leaders taught that the promise would be fulfilled at the end of history, when God would accomplish Israel's salvation through an anointed or chosen king who would be called the messiah or Christ. This kingdom would be called the kingdom of God because it was brought about by the divine plan. The psalms of Solomon indicated that the kingdom would be established in a time of affliction of the Jews by ungodly people, when God would restore justice to Israel. The conditions of the Jews in the first century reflected the conditions of the promise, and the expectations were high for the long awaited messiah. To the confused disciples, Jesus seemed to fit the bill, so it was only fitting to call him "the Christ." It also stimulated the idea that the end of the world was immanent and that Christ would return soon to establish his reign.

INTERPRETATIONS OF THE DEATH AND RESURRECTION

Expiation for Sin

The Hellenistic world was familiar with literature that depicted innocent heroes whose death brought exaltation for themselves and atonement for others. The Roman writer Lucan extolls the death of young Cato, who says in his death throes, "This my blood will ransom all the people; this my death will achieve atonement for all the Romans have deserved for their moral decline" (Fiddes, 1989, p. 67). The Jewish festival of Yom Kippur depicted the need for Jews to atone for the sins they committed during the year. The disciples, in looking for an explanation of the scandalous death of Jesus, claimed that he died for sins, emphasizing his role in salvation. Jesus had said that he came "to give his life as ransom for many" (Mk. 10:45).

The first letter to Timothy says that Jesus Christ was a "mediator between God and humanity... who gave his life as a ransom for all" (1 Tim. 2:5). The usual meaning of ransom is a price paid to obtain the freedom of someone who is held captive. Paul says that by Christ's death "we are set free from the captivity of sin and fear of death" (Rom. 8:21). The idea of ransom as connected to liberation was found in the Hebrew Bible. Ransom was used to describe God's saving act of liberating the Jews from Egypt and Babylon and bringing them into fullness of life. Because their slavery was viewed as the result of their sinfulness, liberation included freedom from the slavery of sin.

One of the purposes of animal sacrifice in ancient Israel was to make the people more acceptable to God by expiating their sin. The sacrifice was an outward symbol of their inner conversion, not that God needed the blood of animals for satisfaction. Paul makes the connection between God's forgiveness of sin of the ancient Jews and the expiatory sacrifice of Jesus. "All are justified by the free gift of his grace, being set free in Christ Jesus" (Rom. 3:24). Paul is very direct: "Christ died for our sins" (1 Cor. 15:3). The interpretation of his death as a sacrifice has been tied to the sacrifices of the paschal lambs. Jesus was described by John the Baptist as the "Lamb of God who takes away the sins of the world" (Jn. 1:29). The image of the victorious Lamb is represented frequently in the Book of Revelation.

Peter Abelard, a theologian from the twelfth century, stressed the element of love as motivation for Christ's death. Death became the consequence of Jesus' own self-sacrificing ministry: "Greater love has no man than this, that a man lay down his life for his friends" (Jn. 15:13). Jesus shows the Christian how to live as well as how to die. His life was a series of sacrifices for others that logically culminated in the total sacrifice of his death. Both his life and death were motivated by love—love of the Father and love for all those he served.

In looking back at their scriptures, the early Christians could find many references that they thought pertained to Jesus as the expected messiah, but it was the title Son of Man that seemed most relevant. Mark (10:45) uses that title in referring to Jesus: "The Son of Man did not come to be served, but to serve and give his life to redeem many." Jesus is identified in Acts (7:55) as the Son of Man, who will return in power and glory. He will not only return but also will come down from heaven (Jn. 3:13). The prophet Daniel had referred to a future time when a figure "Like to a son of man" would come on a cloud and receive the power to judge from an ancient one (Dan. 7:13). After the resurrection Luke says that Jesus was taken up to heaven and a cloud hid him from the sight of the believers. Then "Two men dressed in white stood besides them and said, 'Galileans, why are you standing there looking up to the sky? This Jesus who was taken from you into heaven, will come back in the same way that you saw him go to Heaven'" (Acts 1:11). The expectation of Jesus' immanent return was coupled with the expectation that the end would come soon and the Son of Man would establish his kingdom.

SUMMARY

It is important to locate Jesus of Nazareth in time and place in order to verify his historical existence. Two of the gospel writers give accounts of his birth which are referred to as the infancy narratives. Because the two accounts do not agree in all details, scripture scholars look for the theological meanings that underlie the stories. Little is known of Jesus' childhood, but some authors say he was educated and plied a trade that would place him the middle class of his society. Jesus appeared to be an itinerant preacher who attracted a large group of followers. His preaching centered on the kingdom of God which included everyone, including the poor, outcasts, women and other marginal groups and extended from this world into the future.

Jesus' preaching was accompanied by miracles that were usually done for the powerless in society. Not all of the miracles have the same significance to many theologians, but they do agree that something happened that was unusual enough to cause the stories to be passed on over the years. Jesus used parables to teach the message of the kingdom because they focus on human life and the ways that humans relate to each other. He used metaphors in these parables to illustrate the forgiveness and compassion of God.

Jesus taught a morality that has been called by some a radical ethic because it went so far beyond the traditional codes that regulated human behavior. He said that evil resided in the inner attitude of humans that motivated the action as well as in the overt behavior. His teaching on forgiveness went beyond the Mosaic code of laws. His law of love seemed to offend the religious authorities because it took priority over some of the Talmudic laws of resting on the Sabbath. The night before he died, he called his disciples to celebrate a meal. After the meal and his prayer in the garden, Jesus was arrested and taken to a trial by the Romans on the charge that he wanted to be king. He was found guilty by Pontius Pilate and condemned to death by crucifixion, a horrible, painful ordeal meted out by the Romans to escaped slaves and criminals.

Jesus might have been forgotten if it were not for his having been raised from the dead. His disciples claimed that he appeared on the earth after the resurrection in a transformed existence that transcended time and space. The resurrection became the core doctrinal teaching of Paul, who gave hope to all the disciples that they too, would rise from the dead as their leader did. The evangelists portray the disciples as treating the risen Jesus as God by worshipping him. They called him the Christ or the anointed one and considered him a savior. They applied to Jesus the titles and devotion that they had reserved for God alone.

After the resurrection, Jesus' followers looked for an explanation of his scandalous death. By examining the scriptures of their Hebrew Bible, they found prophecies of the coming messiah which they thought were fulfilled by Jesus. They applied to Jesus the Jewish idea of sacrifice and expiation for sin as an explanation for his death. Looking back at the book of Daniel, they saw Jesus as the celestial Son of Man who would return at the end of time.

DISCUSSION QUESTIONS

1. Why is it important for writers outside the Christian tradition to acknowledge the person of Jesus?
2. How did Jesus explain the time of the kingdom? How do you interpret the kingdom and why?
3. Why are the ethics taught by Jesus considered radical? Give some examples.
4. What were some of the effects of Jesus' choice to serve the marginalized in his society? Are these same conditions present in society today? Why do people today engage in ministry to those on the fringe of society?
5. Why do Christians continue the tradition of the Last Supper?
6. Why was Jesus put to death? How was his death the logical outcome of his life?
7. Give some reasons why you think that the resurrection should or should not hold such a central position in Christian teaching.
8. In what ways did the disciples' experience of the risen Lord affect their understanding of the historical Jesus?
9. Do you think Jesus was a revolutionary who tried to overthrow the Roman Government? Explain your position.
10. Was Jesus a Pharisee who tried to interpret the Talmud?
11. Do you think Jesus used sorcery when driving out devils from possessed persons?
12. Do you think the disciples stole the body of Jesus and then claimed that he had resurrected from the dead?

WORKS CITED

Bredin, Eamonn. *Rediscovering Jesus.* Mystic, CT: Twenty Third Publications, 1986.

Crosson, Dominic. *Jesus.* San Francisco: Harper, 1994.

Feldman, L. H. *Antiquities of the Jews.* Cambridge, MA: Harvard University Press, 1927 (reprinted 1965–67, 18.63–64).

Fiddes, Paul. *Past Event and Present Salvation.* Atlanta: John Knox, 1989.

Kee, Howard, et al. *Christianity: A Social and Cultural History,* Second Edition. Upper Saddle River, NJ: Prentice Hall, 1998.

Kee, Howard. *Medicine, Miracles and Magic in New Testament Time.* New York: Cambridge University Press, 1986.

McGrath, Alister. *An Introduction to Christianity.* Cambridge: Blackwell, 1997.

Meier, John. *A Marginal Jew, Rethinking the Historical Jesus.* New York: Doubleday, 1991.

Nolan, Albert. *Jesus Before Christianity.* Maryknoll, NY: Orbis, 1992.

Perkins, Pheme. *Hearing the Parables of Jesus.* Ramsey, NJ: Paulist Press, 1981.

Perrin, Norman. *Rediscovering the Teaching of Jesus.* New York: Harper and Row, 1967.

Sloyan, Gerard. *Jesus in Focus.* Mystic, CT: Twenty Third Publications, 1983.

Chapter 4

The Early Church

o you believe that Jesus planned to found a church? Do women have the same opportunities as men to attain important positions in Christian churches today? Do you think that Americans today would espouse a cause that they would willingly die for? Your ideas on these questions may become more focused as you apply the early church history to your life.

ACTS OF THE APOSTLES:
THE COMMUNITY OF BELIEVERS

Luke, the author of Acts of the Apostles, described the disciples as staying together as a group, meeting together, and awaiting the return of the Lord. The apostles who were included in the group of disciples were often called the twelve, which appears as a symbol for the twelve tribes of Israel. Mary Magdalene, Mary the mother of Jesus, and other women disciples who were intimate friends of Jesus and shared his ministry were also part of the group. Luke said that Jesus returned to earth and had appeared to them occasionally for a period of forty days after the resurrection, and now in their loss they gathered together with Peter as their spokesperson. They called themselves an *ecclesia,* the Greek word for an assembly of persons. Ecclesia, in the Acts of the Apostles, meant the local churches, but later in Paul's letters the term grew to include the larger number of churches that comprised Christendom. Whether the church was referred to as local or universal, its members knew themselves to be the community of Jesus, whom they recognized as the messiah who rose from the dead and presently sits at the right hand of God (Acts 2:32–36).

Most of the early Christians were Jews, and Acts portrays the disciples preaching in Jewish synagogues. They went to the temple to say their prayers, using psalms from the Old Testament.

The Romans considered them a sect, or small group within the parent religion, Judaism. The connection to Judaism was apparent in the disciples' experience of the Spirit. They considered the Spirit that they felt so strongly on Pentecost as the same Spirit that was sent by God to the prophets of Israel. Peter's speech after his Pentecostal experience reflects the connection to the Jewish prophet Joel, who said in reference to Yahweh, "I will pour out my spirit on you; your sons and daughters shall prophesy. . . ." (Joel 2:28).

Acts describes the coming of the Spirit upon the disciples, who along with Mary, the mother of Jesus, were gathered together in an upper room. "A strong wind filled the house and they saw what looked like tongues of fire which spread out and touched each person there. They were all filled with the Holy Spirit and began to speak in other languages as the Spirit enabled them to speak" (Acts 2:3–5). There were in Jerusalem many people from countries all over the known world. They could understand the disciples who spoke to them in their own languages. The incident was reminiscent of the dispersion of languages that caused the building of the Tower of Babel to fail. This time the Spirit was able to unite the disparate groups, all of whom understood the message. Peter, filled with the confidence of the Spirit, preached to the assembly that Jesus of Nazareth was Israel's promised messiah who had been put to death and whom God raised to God's right side in heaven. Customarily, Oriental kings kept the heir apparent at their right side and the queen at their left; therefore, Peter's speech indicated that Christ was Son of God and heir to the kingdom. One cannot always rely on the veracity of numbers in scripture, but Luke records that 3,000 persons were baptized that day (Lk. 3:41).

Luke presents an idealized picture of the early church with the disciples' preaching supported by miracles. The community shared their goods with each other so that no one was needy. The group prayed together in the temple, but they gathered for the breaking of the bread in the members' houses. It is thought by some scholars that this was the Eucharistic meal that Jesus told them to do "in memory of me" (Lk. 22:19).

The disciples began to spread the Christian message throughout Jerusalem and to the Jewish settlements in the outlying areas of the diaspora. Luke traces the spread of Christianity from its origin in Israel to the expansion of its gospel into the Gentile world. Luke utilizes the journeys of Paul to describe this expansion in stages until both Jewish and Gentile communities embraced the gospel. Paul, formerly known as Saul, helped to spread the teachings of the risen Christ throughout the Roman Empire. He had been a Pharisee and a former persecutor of Christians until he had a religious experience in which Christ spoke to him. He changed his life to become a missionary for Christ and recorded his efforts in letters to the various churches that he established.

With the increased number of converts, the need for some organization in the group emerged. As in any large groups, roles must be assigned to accomplish their purpose or mission. Acts describes the beginnings of an organization with specified means of arriving at authority.

AUTHORITY IN THE EARLY CHURCH

Both the Acts of the Apostles and letters from Paul depict two forms of authority in the early church. One form was called hierarchal, in that authority rested in a leader and passed downward through middle leaders to the people. The other is often referred to as communitarian, or sometimes charismatic, because the authority came from the Holy Spirit and is shared more equally among the followers. Support for the hierarchial model appears in Acts, where the leadership role is assigned to Peter. He speaks at Pentecost, is miraculously released from jail, performs miracles, and along with John leads the missionary effort to Samaria. Matthew's gospel indicates this prime position when Jesus says to Peter, "You are Peter, and upon this rock I will build my church" (Mt. 16:16). Jesus stated that he would give Peter the keys of the kingdom, and whatever he bound on earth would be bound in heaven.

The apostles, including Paul, followed this hierarchal pattern when they founded churches in which they were in charge or appointed elders to positions of leadership. When the prophet Agabus predicted a famine would occur, "The disciples decided that each of them would send money to help the fellow believers who lived in Judea. They sent the money to the church elders by Barnabas and Saul" (Acts 11:29). Paul asked the elders from the church at Miletus to meet him when he came to visit them. James was in charge of the main church in Jerusalem, assisted by elders who oversaw lesser churches. Deacons were appointed by the apostles to help with the more material activities such as the daily distribution of funds and goods. The apostles did not think that they should neglect the preaching of God's word in order to handle finances. So they directed the community to "choose seven men among you who are known to be full of the Holy Spirit and wisdom, and we will put them in charge of this matter" (Acts 6:3). After naming the men, "the group presented them to the apostles, who prayed and placed their hands on them" (Acts 6:6). Later letters from the first century to Timothy and Titus describe the qualifications necessary for church leaders and deacons.

Rather than authority passing downward from Christ to the apostles, elders, and deacons in the hierarchal mode, the communitarian or charismatic form of authority stresses the gifts of the Holy Spirit given to each member. Acts also describes the authority of the prophets, who, although not members of the hierarchy, place their hands on Barnabas and Paul and send them off to preach the word of God. Women could be prophets also, as were the virgin daughters of Philip the deacon "who proclaimed God's message" (Acts 21:9). Paul's letters refer to gifts of the Spirit, called charisms, which are to be used to build up the church. Using the image of the body to underscore the importance of each part that could not function without the other parts, Paul says that each person is to use the gift that God has given them. "If our gift is to speak God's message, we should do it according to our faith; if it is to serve, we should serve, if it is to teach, we should teach, if it is to encourage, we should do so" (Rom. 12:4). He does seem to prioritize these gifts to the Corinthians when he says, "The apostles are in first place; the prophets in second; third, teachers; then those who perform miracles; and lastly those blessed with the gift of tongues" (1 Cor. 12:27).

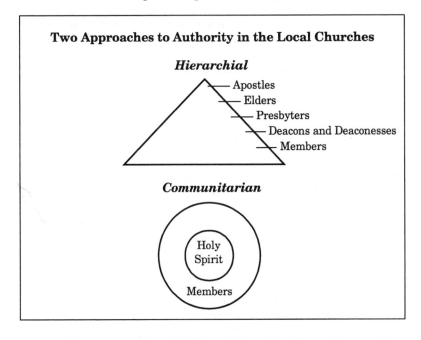

Two Approaches to Authority in the Local Churches

Hierarchial

— Apostles
— Elders
— Presbyters
— Deacons and Deaconesses
— Members

Communitarian

Holy
Spirit

Members

A charismatic group of widows did good works, such as making clothes for the poor. Peter raised one of their members from the dead, a woman named Dorcas, and presented her alive to them. Some scholars think the widows might have been the forerunners of women religious or nuns. The early Christians met in house churches to celebrate the Lord's supper. The owner of the house in which they met was the usual celebrant as host or hostess, which reflected the communitarian dimension of authority. There is no mention of church elders present at these house churches. It was customary for the early Christians to meet in homes for their rituals because they had no churches at that time.

Although both forms of authority, hierarchial and charismatic, existed together in the early church, the hierarchial form emerged as the predominate one. By A.D. 49 a council of apostles and elders was called in Jerusalem to settle the important matter of whether the Gentile converts to Christianity must become Jews first. The church in Jerusalem led by James thought that since the first Christians were Jews, all new members should become Jews before becoming Christians. Peter and Paul had been spreading the good news to the Jews in the outlying areas of the empire. Gentiles were impressed with the ethical behavior of these Jews and became friends with them. When these Jews from the diaspora or the areas outside Israel became Christians, some of the Gentiles did also. However some Gentiles did not want to become Jews first. Adult men did not willingly desire to submit to circumcision or to some of the other strict laws of Judaism. The Greek women enjoyed more freedom than some of their Jewish sisters and were not eager to relinquish it. Peter and Paul led the movement to allow entrance of these Gentiles into the church without becoming Jews first.

The council of Jerusalem agreed to this proposal, which altered the face of Christianity forever. The early Christians no longer were viewed as a sect within Judaism but began the Gentile church that spread over the known world. The communitarian or spirit-led dimension of the church was not ignored, even though it was a meeting of apostles and elders. James, the leader of the church of Jerusalem where the meeting occurred, gave the consensual declaration, "The Holy Spirit and we have agreed not to put any other burden on you" (Acts 15:28). They had agreed that the burdens of the laws of Judaism would not be imposed on the Gentile converts, and entrance into Christianity did not necessitate becoming Jewish first.

The churches outside of Jerusalem that incorporated the Gentiles became organized in a hierarchal manner with their own bishops, presbyters, and male and female deacons. New members entered these churches by baptism rather than by Jewish birth. As the number of these churches grew, a new dimension was added to the concept of church. With so many local churches emerging in various towns and cities, the concept of church took on a more universal perspective as a collection of local churches.

The hierarchal mode of authority predominates in the writings of the later-first and early-second centuries. The letters of John show concern over those preachers who were spreading false doctrine and designated the need for someone in authority to correct them. The later letters of Paul, which scholars believe he did not write although they were attributed him, are Colossians, Ephesians, Timothy, and Titus. These letters describe the necessity to protect the true and correct belief of the Christian message. Sound doctrine is stressed, and warnings are given against faddish and deceitful teachings that are opposed to the eternal truths taught by the church (Eph. 4:13). In order to guard against the distortion of Christian teaching, strong leadership is required. The letters of Timothy and Titus describe levels of authority within the institutional church. The overseer, or bishop, constitutes the highest authority in the local church, followed by elders and deacons. The widows are mentioned as a distinct group with a definite role in the congregation, but it is difficult to see how they fit into the hierarchal institution.

During the latter part of the first and early part of the second century, a body of writings emerged that scholars call the writings of the Apostolic Fathers. These writings emphasized the teaching leadership of bishops, whose duty it was to protect true doctrine. These writings claimed that bishops' authority reached back through the apostles to Jesus. Clement of Rome, its reigning bishop in the latter part of the first century, wrote about the concept of apostolic succession. He said that God appointed the apostles who received the gospel from Christ. After their death, other approved men appointed by the church would succeed them and continue their mission. The *Didache,* or *The Teaching of the Twelve Apostles,* described some of the characteristics desirable in those persons to be appointed bishops and deacons. Polycarp and Ignatius, both bishops, wrote of the necessity of obedience to bishops, who were appointed by God, and to the presbytery, a group of elders holding responsibility for universal church decisions. They also defined true doctrine against false teachings arising around the nature of Christ. The hierarchal mode of authority was developed in order to secure orthodox doctrine and to maintain order in the church, based on the teaching and authority of the apostles, but the gifts of the Spirit were not ignored.

Both forms of authority have endured over the years in various Christian denominations. Roman and Orthodox Catholics and some mainline Protestant denominations, such as Episcopalians, Methodists, and Lutherans, utilize the hierarchal mode when making decisions. Most independent churches, those not belonging to the Council of Churches, such as Pentecostal, Holiness, and Gospel Tabernacle churches, employ the communitarian model where consensus usually reigns. Some denominations, such as Presbyterian, are organized around a combination of both models, with decisions made by a presbytery or a board of trustees, who are often pastors of local churches.

WOMEN IN EARLY CHRISTIANITY

One must approach the role of women as depicted in the scriptures carefully, noting the androcentric (from the male point of view) interpretations of the New Testament. Because the scriptures are written from the experience of men in a patriarchal culture, women often appear marginal or in lesser positions. Contemporary women biblical scholars, such as Elizabeth Schussler Fiorenza, have examined their scriptures closely to find the examples of women who had prominent positions in the New Testament church. Their work is challenging because of some of the conflicting statements by Paul regarding women. In some cases he upholds them and considers them coworkers in his missionary endeavors. At other times, he consigns women to secondary or even subservient positions, telling them to be silent in church. The Acts of Apostles appears to support women in that Luke shows them positively engaged in ministry. For example, he mentions Dorcas and the widows who care for the poor, the prophetesses, and the women whose churches meet in their homes.

The owners of the homes where the house churches met became the acknowledged leaders of the community which met on their property. Besides the Christian community that met in the house of the mother of John Mark (Acts 12:12), Paul cites house churches that met in the homes of Lydia, Nympha, and Prisca or Priscilla. The house of Priscilla still stands outside of Rome, Italy, over the catacombs that held the graves of the Christian martyrs. A chapel in the catacombs that dates back to the first century A.D. has a fresco on the wall that depicts seven women sharing what appears to be a Eucharistic meal. Until recently, in the latter part of this century, the fresco appeared to depict seven men instead of women. Some women art historians noticed that someone had painted beards and men's clothing over the images of the women. They peeled off the paint to reveal the true identity of the participants.

The patriarchal influence of later centuries also defaced a mosaic found in the church of St Praxedes in Rome. A mosaic of a woman found along the side of the door frame depicts a woman with the inscription "Theodore, Episcopus." The male name Theodore, and the Latin male term for bishop, *episcopus,* had the last letters of their words in a different color mosaic than the rest of the letters. Whoever tampered with the letters forgot to change the words across the door post that still say, "Theodora, Episcopa," the Latin feminine form of bishop. Joan Morris (1973), an art historian, claims that this mosaic supports the position of women as bishops in the early church (p. 66).

Acts depicts a husband-and-wife team, Priscilla and Aquila, who were engaged in a teaching and preaching ministry (Acts 18:1–3, 24–26). Because Priscilla's name precedes her husband's, many scholars think that she was more prominent in the ministry. Mary Magdalene is considered an apostle by many because she fits the description of an apostle—witness to the resurrection of Christ and sent to preach it. All the gospels depict her as arriving first at the empty tomb of Jesus and being commissioned by the angels to tell the other apostles of Jesus' resurrection.

Ambiguity of Paul

Paul has at times been most supportive of women in the ministry of the early church. In his letter to the Philippians (4:2–3), Paul mentions two women, Euodia and Syntyche, "who struggled together with me for the gospel along with Clement and the rest of my coworkers." Ben Witherington (1990), a scripture scholar, says that the key verb "struggle," is drawn from athletic terminology at pagan games and gladiatorial matches and could easily be translated as "fought together side by side." "This hardly suggests a passive role in spreading the gospel, but rather one that involved real activity, difficult struggles and noteworthy sacrifices" (p. 186). Language translators have confused some interpretations of Paul's reference to Phoebe in his letter to the Romans (16:1). He is asking the Christian community to support her and calls her "Diakonos," a term Paul used 22 times in his writings. Translators of the King James version of the Bible interpreted it 18 times as *minister*, three times as *deacon*, and only here as *servant*: "Phoebe serves the church at Cenechrae." Russell Prohl (1957), a language specialist, says that Diakonos can mean "full-fledged pastors, preachers and evangelists" (p. 69). It can also mean one who presides, a ruler or a leader. It appears that Phoebe not only served the church at Cenechrae, but she could have been the leader in charge of the Christian community. In referring to this text, Origen, an outstanding thinker of the third century, said, "This text teaches with the authority of the Apostle. . . there are women deacons in the church, and that women who have given assistance to so many people, and who by their good works deserve to be praised by the Apostle, ought to be accepted into the diaconate" (quoted in Gryson, 1976, p. 134).

Women seem to be among Paul's most reliable coworkers involved in spreading the Christian message. In his letter to the Romans, he refers to Junia, who along with her husband was "outstanding among the apostles" (16:7). Paul calls Mary, Trypaena, and Tryphosa his coworkers, indicating that these women likely acted as missionaries, conducted worship services that met at their houses, and performed charitable works. By referring to both men and women as his coworkers, Paul underscores the egalitarian structure of the early church. He does not attribute lower or higher authority to men or women but considers them equals. The gospel message was entrusted to both men and women, who spread it not only by word but also by example. Belief in the message of Christ transcended the boundaries of social class, gender, and race. Paul wrote, "For as many of you as were baptized into Christ have put on Christ. There is neither Jew nor Greek, there is neither slave nor free, there is neither male nor female, you are all one in Christ" (Gal. 3:27–28). More than belief, Paul wrote of the practice of allowing men and women, Jew and Gentile, slave and free to worship together and experience the fellowship of the Christian community.

Although Paul seemed at times so supportive of women, he also seemed in other instances to keep them in subordinate positions. He said, "Man is the image of God's glory and women are the reflection of man's glory" (1 Cor. 11:19). He also told women to be subject to their husbands because Christ is head of the church and the husband is head of the wife. He suggested that women wear veils to signify this submission. Later in this same letter, he tells women that they "must be silent in church" (1 Cor. 14:3–4). The real change in his attitude toward women appears in the pastoral letters, which, although attributed to Paul, were written at least thirty years after his death. Letters addressed to Titus and Timothy written in the second century designate the qualifications of bishops and helpers who are all male. Women are told not to be slanderers nor slaves to wine. They must love their husbands and children, "be self controlled and pure, submit themselves to their husbands, so that no one will speak evil of the message that comes from God" (Titus 2:5). The patriarchal tendencies of the second century chose to ignore the positive affirmation given by Paul to women and focused on the secondary position assigned to them by male leaders.

As the Christians grew in numbers, they began to penetrate the Roman world. In the beginning, the early members attracted persons from the lower classes of society. But in Paul's lifetime, the membership expanded to include the upper classes. Paul wrote to his friend Philemon encouraging him to take back his slave, Onesimus, and treat him as a brother. Paul had converted a wealthy woman named Lydia, and all her household. Luke tells us that the apostles were making many converts to Christianity, which raised questions regarding Jewish loyalty. The situation became one that instigated persecution, first by the Jewish leaders and then the Romans.

CHRISTIANITY AS A MINORITY RELIGION

Oppression by the Jewish Leaders

Many converts were joining the Christians (recall Luke's assertion that 3,000 persons were baptized and added to their number in one day). "Day by day the Lord added to their community those destined to be saved" (Acts 2:41). Although scholars warn that numbers in biblical writings cannot always be taken literally, Luke asserts, "The total number of men had now risen to something like 5,000" (Acts 4:4). Peter and John were arrested because they taught that Jesus was raised from the dead, which was in opposition to the teachings of the Sadducees. The chief priests, scribes, and other members of the Sanhedrin, the governing body of the Jews, warned the apostles never to teach in the name of Jesus.

Luke records that so many miracles were done by the apostles that the sick were taken into the streets so that Peter's shadow might fall on the ill and cure them. People from nearby towns came to Jerusalem seeking cures of the sick, as well as those tormented by unclean spirits. Luke attributes jealousy as the motive that caused the Jewish leaders to arrest the apostles. Peter and John miraculously escaped from jail and were preaching in the temple when they were arrested again. After an intervention by a respected Jewish teacher, Gamaliel, the apostles were flogged and released with the warning never to speak in the name of Jesus. The apostles, rejoicing that they were so honored to suffer humiliation for Jesus, continued to preach in the temple and in private homes. Stephen, a deacon, was stoned to death for his impassioned preaching about Jesus as messiah. Saul, who later became Paul, approved of his murder and joined in a more systematic attack on the Christians. Saul went from house to house arresting men and women and sending them to jail. He was on his way to Damascus to arrest Christians when he had his conversion experience and dedicated the rest of his life to spreading the Christian message.

The persecution in Jerusalem culminated in the death of James, the leader of the Jerusalem church. James and some followers were seized by the high priest Ananus and brought before the Sanhedrin, where they were condemned to death by stoning. The persecution by the Jewish leaders continued, driving many of the Jewish converts out to the surrounding areas. The Jewish leaders tried to kill Paul, but he escaped when he made it known to the Roman tribune that he was a Roman citizen (Acts 26:21).

John's gospel discloses antagonism between the Jewish Christians and the religious Jews who were faithful to their heritage. Christians' devotion to Christ as God offended the Jewish belief in monotheism, which only allowed worship of the one God, Yahweh. After the destruction of Jerusalem in A.D. 70, Christians moved the center of their religious activity to Rome. Their full break with Judaism was marked by celebrating Sunday instead of Saturday as the Sabbath or Lord's Day, and by eating the Lord's supper as their main ritual meal each week instead of the Jewish meal performed once a year at Passover time. But Christians retained much of their Jewish heritage, including the Jewish scriptures and congregational prayer.

Oppression by the Romans

The Romans persecuted the Christians for refusing to offer sacrifice to their gods. Roman authorities demanded proof that their citizens performed this ritual with a signed certificate by the Roman official who witnessed the action. An example of the certificate is presented here.

To: The Commissioners for Sacrifices in the village of Alexander Island

From : Aurelius Diogenes, son of Sabatus

Re: A 72 year old man, from the village of Alexander's Island with a scar on his right eyebrow.

I have always sacrificed to the gods. Now, in your presence, in accordance with the terms of the edict, I have offered a sacrifice, poured libations, and tasted the sacrifices. I request you to certify to this effect. Farewell.

Presented by me, Aurelius Diogenes, I certify that I witnessed his sacrifice.

Aurelius Syrus

Although the Romans allowed many sects and various religious movements within their empire, most of them adhered to the polytheism of the Roman religion. When the emperor Domitian (A.D. 81–96) demanded to be addressed as Lord and God, these groups did not hesitate to offer sacrifice and obedience to him. Christians who refused to offer sacrifices to Roman gods or humans began to suffer persecution because they were perceived as disloyal to the state. The Roman emperors built large structures where the people were called upon to gather in solemn assemblies. They showed their devotion to the gods and to the state by offering sacrifices and participating in ceremonies at these obligatory sessions.

The Emperor Trajan (98–117) answered a letter from his governor in Asia Minor, Pliny, regarding the behavior of Christians who failed to attend these assemblies. Pliny said that the Christians did nothing subversive; they met on Sundays to sing, pray, eat a meal together, and take oaths against violence. They worshipped a god called Christus but refused to repeat an invocation to the Roman gods or to offer adoration with sacrifice to the image of the emperor. Christians who refused this worship were put to death. Trajan told Pliny to continue this policy, but not to seek Christians out or seize them without proper evidence. These persecutions continued sporadically throughout the empire, reaching a climax during the reign of the emperor Decius who was killed in 251. One of the most severe persecutions occurred under the emperor Diocletian in 303. He issued an edict to destroy all Christian places of worship and all their books. Christian civil servants were reduced to slaves, and prominent Christians were forced to offer sacrifices to the emperor. The emperor Galerius ordered the cessation of the persecution in 311, but it was not until the reign of the Emperor Constantine in 313 that Christianity was recognized as a religion.

Christians themselves faced a crisis of faith because they were expecting the immanent return of Jesus. They remembered the words of Jesus as recorded by Mark, "Truly this generation will not pass away before these things take place" (Mk. 13:30). Many of the first Christians did pass away without seeing "The Son of Man coming on clouds in great power and glory" (Mk. 13:36). By the sixties of the first century a whole generation had died and still the Parousia or Second Coming of Christ had not occurred. Coupled with the persecution by the Roman state, this failed expectation caused some Christians to question their commitment to their religion. The delay of the Parousia and the martyrdom of the believers caused some Christians to apostatize or recant from their commitment, while others remained steadfast in their devotion to Christianity.

Christians had models of steadfast devotion to Christ in their leaders. Paul was summoned to Rome, where he was beheaded around A.D. 64 for his teachings about Christ. Nero blamed Christians for the fire in Rome and in A.D. 65 launched a persecution against them. Some of them were torn to pieces in the arena by wild animals, and others he had crucified in his garden and then set on fire "to illuminate the night when daylight failed" (Tacitus, Annals 15:44, 1989 ed.). Peter became an example of one whose courage in the face of martyrdom began to waiver. He was persuaded by the brethren to leave Rome because he was being sought for execution. Legend says that as he left the city in disguise, he met the Lord on the road about to enter the city. Peter asked him where he was going, and the Lord answered that he was going to be crucified. Peter could not understand how Christ could be crucified again until he realized that it was himself that should return to the city for his own execution. Peter was crucified upside down at his own request because he did not think himself worthy to die in the same way as Jesus. On the cross Peter exhorted the Christians to keep their faith in Christ and not to fear death in his name. Christians who witnessed the courageous deaths of three of their leaders, James, Paul and Peter, tried to follow their example and stay loyal to their belief in Christ in spite of his delay in returning.

Besides the zeal of the martyrs, some basic Christian beliefs and practices caused them to expand throughout the empire. Upper-class Romans, such as Erastus, the city treasurer at Corinth, and Pomponia Graecina, a woman of the senatorial class, were attracted to their number. Marta Sordi (1986), a church historian, says, "We know from reliable sources that there were Christians among the aristocracy in the second half of the first century" (p. 28). Many artisans, merchants, and even soldiers were joining the group, but often it was the women who converted their husbands and families. Some upper-class women who were attracted to Christianity converted their husbands, who as masters of the house had all their servants and slaves baptized also. The Romans had practiced female infanticide, which left a shortage of women of childbearing age. Jack Kinsay, a sociologist, reports that even in large Roman families "more than one daughter was never reared." Kinsay found that inscriptions at Delphi showed that out of six hundred families, only six had raised more than one daughter (Stark, 1996, p. 68). Christians objected to abortions and female infanticide, which raised the birth rate in the Christian subculture.

Another practice that increased the number of Christians was their witness to their love for one another. Two large epidemics killed many inhabitants of the Roman world. The first one in A.D. 165 started with the military in the East and then spread throughout the empire. The second one in the third century killed as many as 5,000 people a day in the city of Rome (McNeill, 1976). The Roman pagans let their sick die and would leave them alone without treatment out of fear of contamination. They saw the Christians nurse their sick, feed them, and bury their dead, while the pagans just left their dead to rot. The pagan priests and influential leaders would flee the cities while the Christians, both leaders and members, braved disease to care for their loved ones. The survival rate among Christians was much higher than among pagans, which caused the pagans to view the Christians with admiration. When the Christians would nurse even the pagans, living out their commandment of love, more converts were made, increasing the number of Christians in the empire.

As the persecutions continued into the second century, the first persons to suffer martyrdom were the leaders such as the bishops and deacons. Ignatius of Antioch said that he was happy to suffer his body to be ground up by the wild beasts, just as the wheat is ground to form the bread of the body of Christ. Polycarp, the Bishop of Smyrna, was burned alive and his bones recovered by the Christians to be venerated.

Women as well as men were sent to the arena to be killed by wild animals for the spectacle of the Roman audience. Perpetua of Carthage left in her diary the scene of a group of Christians being led into the arena to be killed in 203. They were smiling and singing hymns praising God. Perpetua herself was destined for martyrdom. After the torture of being thrown onto the horns of a wild cow, both Perpetua and a slave woman, Felictas, were killed by the sword. Thecla was thrown to wild beasts, but the lioness protected her by killing the attacking bear. When Thecla threw herself into a pond of wild seals with the intent of baptizing herself, the seals floated about, dead, unable to attack her. Agnes was a beautiful young girl whose hand was sought in marriage by the son of a Roman official. She had promised herself to Christ and so she refused his proposal. She was humiliated by his offended father, who forced her to walk naked through the streets. Her hair miraculously grew to cover her body, which she took as a sign that Christ accepted her offer. Agnes was finally beheaded while saying prayers of thanksgiving that she could be wed to Christ. The bravery and determination of the martyrs attracted the admiration of many pagans who became Christians.

RESPONSE OF CHRISTIAN THINKERS

While the martyrs were spreading the Christian message through the sacrifice of their lives, Christian thinkers were reacting to the accusations made against them intellectually. Philosophy was highly esteemed by the Romans and the Greeks. Christian intellectuals had to show the pagans that Christianity was a respectable philosophical system in order to gain their regard. Christians had to answer some of the accusations made against them, such as atheism, cannibalism, and political subversion. Four outstanding Christian thinkers who wrote extensively to defend the Christian faith are Justin, Clement, Origen, and Tetullian.

Justin Martyr (100–165)

After exploring the philosophy of Aristotle, Plato, and the Stoics, Justin became a convert to Christianity. Justin described Christianity as a rational search for truth and invited critics to dialogue about it on philosophical grounds. Justin compared Jesus' teaching with that of the ancient philosophers who motivated the populace to moral living. He said that Christians pray for their enemies, and if nonbelievers lived according to Christ's precepts, they would receive the same reward from God who governs everyone. Justin defended philosophically the premise that God of the Christian scriptures and God of the Greek and Roman philosophers were the same. Using the Greek word *logos* to illustrate the power of divine reason, he appealed to the intelligentsia who could understand the logos as implanting divine wisdom or the seed of truth in all human beings. This logos revealed itself to the Greek philosophers as it did to the prophets of the Old Testament. Then the logos became flesh in the person of Jesus Christ, who continues to instill wisdom in his followers. Now everyone, Christians and non-Christians alike, can participate in the wisdom of God as taught by Jesus Christ.

Justin did get into trouble with the Romans, because although Christians were willing to pay taxes to the state, they would not offer sacrifice to the emperor or renounce their allegiance to Christ. As a result, he and the others on trial with him were put to death for their faith in God and their refusal to honor the emperor as divine.

Clement of Alexandria (150–211) Prof.

Alexandria was known for its catechetical school that instructed converts to Christianity and educated followers to greater understanding of their religion. Clement became head of this school after his own conversion to Christianity. Although persecution of Christians was occurring sporadically throughout the empire, this school flourished. Clement appealed to the intellectuals by using the logos term to uphold the unity and eternity of God. Jesus, who was God, became human in order to instruct humans how to live in obedience to God. He challenged the Roman scholars by declaring that faith was superior to knowledge. He said that faith leads one to that superior knowledge that is infused by God. Through this inspiration humans can arrive at a better knowledge of God and things spiritual than they ever could attain by mere study. During the persecution by the emperor Decius (193–211), Clement was forced to flee from Egypt to Cappadocia in Asia Minor, where he died.

Origen (185–283) Theologion / Bishop

After the death of his father, who was martyred under the emperor Severus, Origen headed the catechetical school in his native Alexandria. His love of study of both secular and sacred subjects led to this appointment when he was only eighteen years old. He tried to show the correlation between Greek philosophy and sacred scripture. His commentaries on the Bible sought to make applications to everyday Christian living. Origen compared the morally superior teachings of Jesus to the morally debased practices of the Greek and Roman gods and goddesses in his effort to justify Christianity. He contrasted the power of Jesus with the power of the Roman empire in that Christianity spread throughout the Roman Empire in spite of Roman official opposition. He said that from the lowly origins of unlettered people in Palestine, Jesus' teachings transcended ethnic and social class boundaries to convert kings, Roman senators, and common people. Jesus, with a human body, points to the reality of God incarnate in human form, thereby elevating the whole person—body and intellect. Origen taught that God cared for all rational beings but expected them to use their decision-making ability for good moral purposes. They would be held accountable for their actions and could expect divine judgment if they strayed from what they knew was right. His outspoken efforts to transform the cultural and intellectual forces of the Roman world brought him torture and death under the emperor Decius.

Tertullian (155–225) lawyer

Tertullian wrote in Latin, the language of commoners, rather than Greek, which was the language of intellectuals. In defense of the accusations that Christians were subversive, he described what Christians really did, giving a detailed description of life in the church of the second century. He said that Christians gathered to pray to God for strength and guidance, for the welfare of the emperor and the state, and for peace. They held members accountable for their actions to be consistent with the teachings of Jesus, and if they committed grievous errors, they were excommunicated. Financial and human support were given to the poor, widows, orphans, the sick, and the aged. The community was presided over by a presbyter or elder who provided for by the group. Tertullian gave a good description of the communal ritual of the Eucharist. It included prayers, songs, and a celebration of the last supper and its anticipation of the death of Jesus. In his efforts to protect orthodox teaching, Tertullian promoted adherence to the truths as taught by the apostles. He advocated baptism to be performed in the apostolic tradition, preferably by a bishop after adequate preparation in the faith.

In their efforts to accommodate to the larger world culture, the Christians tried to converse with the philosophers of their time. They had to make the teachings relevant not only to the common folk, but also to the thinkers of the Roman Empire. Yet, the early fathers did not betray or water down the teachings to win converts or to make Christianity a respected philosophy of life. They were challenged to remain true to doctrine as taught by the apostles and yet to present it in such a way that educated Greeks and Romans would accept it. The writings of the early fathers give moderns worthy insights into the problems that the early church had to face, both from within and from without the confines of their communities. One of these problems, which took some years to settle, concerned the person of Jesus.

Constantine (274–337)

Constantine, a leader of the Gauls from the North defeated the Roman military under Maxentius in A.D. 311. He claimed to have had a dream in which he saw a cross and the words, "In this sign you will conquer." Although he did not become Christian until his deathbed, he favored the religion after his victory. He issued an edict from Milan in 313 that gave religious freedom to all religions in the empire. Although Christianity was still a minority religion, the edict gave it the standing of equality with all religions. Constantine declared that all property taken from the Christians be restored and that they have free and unrestricted opportunity of religious worship. After Constantine extended his victory over the Eastern Empire, Christianity became the majority religion.

Constantine saw himself as active in church politics and in the establishment of church doctrine. When treating Christ as God, Christians sometimes gave the impression that they were polytheists believing in two gods, the Father and the Son. In order to clarify their position as belief in one God, Christian leaders struggled to ascertain that the Father and Christ are one God. A serious debate arose regarding the identity of Jesus. One group claimed that Jesus was only human, a creature of God. Constantine called a council of church leaders at Nicea in 325 that proclaimed that the Father and Son are one being.

The formula produced by the council is called the Nicene Creed. Eusebius of Caesarea recorded the following version:

> We believe in One God, the Father Almighty, maker of all things, visible and invisible, and in one Lord Jesus Christ the Son of God, the only begotten of the father, that is from the substance of the father, God of God, Light of Light, true God of true God, begotten, not made, of one substance with the Father, through whom all things were made, both in heaven and on earth, and for our salvation descended and became incarnate, becoming human, suffered and rose again on the third day, ascended to the heavens, and will come to judge the living and the dead.

THE SEARCH FOR UNDERSTANDING
THE NATURE OF CHRIST

It took until 451 at a Council at Chalcedon to declare that Christ was one person with two natures, one human and one divine. Modern Christians have shown an interest in trying to ascertain just how this is possible—how can Jesus Christ be both human and divine? Most Christians agree to the premise that Christ possessed two natures in the one person, although there is some division over the way it was accomplished.

Christologies

Just as the study of the psyche is called psychology, the study of Christ's unique combination of a human and divine nature is called Christology. There are a variety of ways to understand the presence of God in Christ, but the most prominent are Incarnational Christology, sometimes referred to as Christology from above, and Exaltational Christology, sometimes called Christology from below. Some authors such as Robert Kysar (1993) and Gerald O'Collins (1995) see both theologies as complimenting each other and bringing forth a fuller picture of Christ.

Incarnational Theory. The proponents of the Incarnational theory, or Christology from above, say that Christ was with God as the preexistent Son from all eternity and came down from heaven to take on human flesh in the person of Jesus of Nazareth. Jesus is the eternal Word of God in person and the Eternal Son of God, not because of the belief of the followers but because that is in essence what he is. Incarnational theologians cite the prologue of John's gospel, which stresses the eternity of the Word that was with God and the same as God. This eternal word became flesh and dwelt among God's people. McBrien (1996) says, "Christology from above begins with the preexistent word of God in heaven, who comes down to earth to take on human flesh and to redeem us by dying on the cross, rising from the dead, and returning to enjoy an exalted state in heaven" (p. 493). Incarnational theorists also cite Paul, who claims in his letter to the Philippians that Jesus emptied himself of his God nature and took on human nature, even though it caused his death on the cross. The absolute love of God is shown in the often quoted phrase, "God so loved the world that he sent his only beloved son" (Jn. 3:18). Proponents of Incarnational Christology also cite Paul's letter to the Colossians, in which he says that Jesus Christ is "the image of the invisible God, in whom all fullness of God was pleased to dwell" (Col. 1:15,19).

Exaltation Theory. The exaltation theory, or Christology from below, posits the belief that Jesus was born of human parents, Mary and Joseph. He lived a purely human life and experienced all the problems, frustrations, temptations and sufferings that all humans endure. He had to exercise faith in order to undergo the pains of the cross and desertion. He did not know that he was the Son of God, so he did not recognize the significance of many of the events in his life, such as his baptism, miracles, prophesies, or even his death. It was only in the light of the resurrection that his followers applied to him the prophecies of the Hebrew Bible, which they believed pointed to him as messiah and Son of God. Theologians promoting the exultation theory of Christology say that Jesus of Nazareth, although human, was so open and obedient to God that God exalted him to the position of His Son, who now reigns in heaven as God. God raised him from his human nature to that of divinity. Followers of the exultation theory base their conclusions on the synoptic gospels of Matthew, Mark, and Luke, who portray a more human Jesus than does John. Although in their infancy narratives Luke and Matthew write of a virgin birth, most scripture scholars say these are theological constructs. Mark shows a Jesus who comes on the scene as an adult and experiences the human emotions of joy, fear, and anger.

Both theories acknowledge the fundamental truth that Christ is both human and divine. By recognizing Christ as God, Christians consider him worthy of worship, an act not given to humans. Since the inception of Christianity in the first century, Christians have incorporated into ritual the practice of worshipping Christ as God. Even Pliny, in his letter to the emperor Trajan, claims the Christians gathered every Sunday and worshipped Christus, whom they treated as a God. Together both Christologies highlight the truth that Jesus, who was recognized as the Christ, was both human and divine.

SUMMARY

Luke gives an idealized picture of the early Christian church in the Acts of the Apostles. Many Jews joined the group, which appeared to be a sect within Judaism after the Pentecostal experience of the disciples. As the group grew in numbers, a need for organization appeared. Appeal was made to the authority of the apostles to settle disputes and regulate teaching and actions. One form of authority emerged that could be called communitarian or charismatic, in which the Holy Spirit guided the decisions through prophets. The hierarchal form, with authority flowing downward through bishops, elders, and deacons, predominated by the second century. The missionary work of Peter and Paul brought many Gentiles to the new faith. The council of Jerusalem held in A.D. 49 employed both forms of authority when the apostles and elders decided to allow the Gentiles to become Christians without becoming Jews first. Church leaders in early centuries appealed to the authority of the apostles to secure sound doctrine and authentic teachings.

Women held positions of honor and prestige in the early egalitarian church. They represented Paul's teaching that there should be no difference between men and women, slave and free, Jew and Gentile. Both Luke and Paul point to the ministry of women who worked together with men. Paul appears at times ambiguous in his attitude toward women in that he both supports them and then assigns them to secondary positions. The second-century pastoral letters emphasize the position of men in the church at the expense of women.

As the churches increased their numbers, they appeared to threaten the Jewish establishment. Some Jewish leaders began to persecute the apostles and finally had them killed for preaching that Jesus was the messiah. When the Christians began to treat Christ as a God, the Jewish devotion to monotheism was offended. The Romans persecuted the Christians because they refused to offer sacrifice to the Roman emperors or the gods of their religion. Although the persecution was sporadic over 250 years, it was also fierce. The Christians admired the martyrs who gave their lives so willingly for their beliefs. Roman pagans were impressed with the kindness and generosity of the Christians, and more of them converted to Christianity. Upper-class Romans began to convert to the new religion in spite of the persecution that finally ended in 311. The emperor Constantine issued an edict allowing all religions to co-exist and in 313 returned the property confiscated from the Christians.

While the martyrs were defending Christianity with their deaths and other Christians were arousing admiration from their selfless living, Christian thinkers were defending their faith to the intellectuals. Such men as Justin, Clement, Origen, and Tertullian tried to show the intellectual and moral worth of the new faith. In trying to adapt Christianity to the Roman culture, they had to attain the fine line of trying to be relevant without betraying their basic doctrine. One doctrine that challenged Christian thinkers was the identity of Christ. The Council of Nicea defined that he was both human and divine, leaving later theologians to determine how this combination could exist. Today many Christians lean either toward the incarnational or exaltational approach to Christology.

DISCUSSION QUESTIONS

1. What is the significance of the word church? How is it applied to-day?
2. Luke portrays an idyllic Christian community in Acts. What conflicts do you think might have occurred?
3. Why did the disciples expect the immanent return of Christ? How did this expectation affect their beliefs and actions?
4. Describe two modes of arriving at authority in the early church with an advantage and disadvantage for each.
5. The council of Jerusalem illustrates the inclusiveness of the first Christians. How inclusive do you think Christians are today regarding gender, race, and ethnic diversity?
6. How can we say that Paul was ambiguous toward women? In what ways do some Christian churches continue to display ambiguity toward women?
7. Why were the early Christians persecuted by the Jews and Romans? Are there similar motives today for persecution of minority groups?
8. How did the early Christian thinkers promote the growth of Christianity?
9. Which Christology, incarnational or exultational, do you prefer, and why?

WORKS CITED

The Didache [ca. 100], in the *Apostolic Fathers*. Lightfoot, J.B. and J.R. Harmer, eds. Grand Rapids: Baker Book House, 1984.

Eusebius [ca. 325]. *The History of the Church*. Trans. Kirsopp Lake. Loeb Classical Library. Cambridge: Harvard University Press, 1947.

Gryson, Roger. *The Ministry of Women in the Early Church*. Collegeville, MN: Liturgical Press, 1976.

Kysar, Robert. *John the Maverick Gospel*. Louisville, KY: Wesminister/ John Knox, 1993.

Lake, Kirsopp. *The Apostolic Fathers*. Loeb Classical Library. Cambridge: Harvard University Press, 1912.

Lindsay, Jack. *The Ancient World: Manners and Morals*. New York: Putnam's Sons, 1968.

McBrien, Richard. *Catholicism*. San Francisco: Harper, 1996.

McNeill, William. *Plagues and People* Garden City: Doubleday, 1996.

Morris, Joan. *The Lady Was a Bishop*. New York: Macmillan, 1973.

O'Collins, Gerald. *Christology*. New York: Oxford University Press, 1995.

Prohl, Russell. *Women in the Church*. Grand Rapids, MI: Eerdmann, 1957.

Sordi, Marta. *The Christians and the Roman Empire*. Norman: University of Oklahoma Press, 1986.

Stark, Rodney. *The Rise of Christianity.* Princeton: Princeton University Press, 1996.

Witherington, Ben. *Women and the Genesis of Christianity.* Cambridge, England: Cambridge University Press, 1990.

Chapter Five

The Spread
of Christianity

ho were the Christians of the fourth century, and in what areas of the empire did they live? The early Christian missionaries moved through the areas close to Palestine in the eastern part of the empire and then made their way toward the west. They found their first converts from the urban and smaller towns that housed the manual laborers and merchants. The peasants from the countryside who were less receptive to Christianity were called the *Pagani,* or countryfolk, by the Christians. The word pagan is derived from the Roman word for countryfolk. In time, many soldiers who were conscripted into the Roman army from the countryside seemed willing to convert to the religion of their Christian commanders. There were some flourishing Christian communities in the cities of North Africa where bishops ruled the churches of local congregations, providing them with a stable organization of authority and service. It was from these towns and cities that the Emperor Constantine called their bishops to a council to define Christian doctrine.

DOCTRINAL DECISIONS AND CREEDS

With so many Christian communities spread throughout the empire, various interpretations arose regarding theology, beliefs and practices. Belief in the divinity of Christ was central to Christianity, but this doctrine was challenged by the theology of monotheism. If God was God, and Jesus was God, were there not two Gods?

Council of Nicea (325)

One solution to the question was given by a presbyter, Arius, who declared that Christ was not fully human nor fully divine, but there was a time when he was a creature. This would diminish his divinity if he was created by God. He taught that Christ provided a bridge between God and humans. Arius's position caused much dissention in the church because he attracted many followers who disagreed with traditional church teaching regarding the divinity of Christ. For more political than theological reasons, Constantine called the bishops to Nicea in 325 where, in council, they produced the Nicene Creed, which said that Jesus Christ was human and divine. This creed continues to be said in most Christian churches today at their Sunday rituals. Although other creeds were in existence from the time of the gospels (Mt. 28:19) to prepare individuals for baptism, this creed, later completed in the next council of Constantinople, was promulgated to the whole church. It is called the Nicene Creed although it was finished and declared later at Constantinople in A.D. 381.

> We believe in one God, the Father Almighty, maker of heaven and earth, of all that is, seen and unseen. We believe in one Lord, Jesus Christ, the only Son of God, eternally begotten of the Father, God from God, Light from Light, true God from true God, begotten not made, of one being with the Father. Through Him all things were made. For us and our salvation, He came down from heaven, by the power of the Holy Spirit, He became incarnate from the Virgin Mary, and was made man. For our sake He was crucified under Pontius Pilate, He suffered death and was buried. On the third day He arose again according to the scriptures, He ascended into heaven and is seated at the right hand of the Father. He will come again in glory to judge the living and the dead, and his kingdom will have no end. We believe in the Holy Spirit, the Lord and giver of life, who proceeds from the Father and the Son. With the Father and the Son He is worshipped and glorified. He has spoken through the prophets, and in one holy catholic and apostolic church. We acknowledge one baptism for the forgiveness of sins. We look for the resurrection of the dead and the life of the world to come.

The Apostles' Creed is a shortened version of this Nicene Creed and is often said by the faithful at the rituals of Baptism and Confirmation. Both of these creeds underscore the divinity of Christ, because they say that he is of the same substance as God.

Council of Ephesus (431)

The dispute over the nature of Christ led to clarification over the status and role of his mother, Mary. Was she only the mother of the human Christ, or was she also the mother of the divine Christ who was also God? This council, meeting in Ephesus in modern Turkey, said that Jesus could not be separated into two persons, the human Jesus and the divine Christ because he was only one person. Since Mary was the mother of both the human and the divine Jesus, they used the method of philosophical syllogism to arrive at the conclusion that Mary could be called the mother of God.

Mary is the Mother of Jesus.
Jesus is God.
Therefore, Mary is the Mother of God.

When the church taught that Mary was the mother of God, it assigned her a more renowned status eliciting more reverence and devotion from the faithful. The official church claimed that she was only human, not a goddess, but Christians have expressed their devotion to her with prayer and pageantry throughout the centuries.

Council of Chalcedon (451)

In order to emphasize the oneness of God, this council carefully nuanced the two natures of Christ that resided in his one person. They said that the divine nature of Christ was consubstantial (of the same substance or essence) with God the Father and his human nature consubstantial with other humans. This did not cause a division in his personhood because both natures, human and divine, concurred into one substance and one person. Jesus Christ contained within himself the nature of humans and the nature of God. He was truly human and truly divine.

Although these three councils in the fourth and fifth centuries defined a unified doctrine for Christianity, they left to modern theologians to explain just how these two natures reside in the one person, Jesus Christ. The study of Christology, as mentioned in the previous chapter, has tried to answer this question in modern terms.

Identification of Christianity with Roman Civilization

Roman emperors saw the value of religion as a means to consolidate their empire. By the end of the fourth century, the Emperor Theodosius assigned Christianity to the status of state religion. As the official religion of the empire, Christianity began to incorporate many Roman characteristics, such as the imperial form of government, the Latin language, and many aspects of its art and architecture.

Some of the pagan customs and ethics of the Roman peasantry provided a challenge to the Christian missionaries. Many of the pagans applied the law of vengeance to their enemies and held little regard for women. For example, female infants were sometimes left outside in the elements to die because they would not make good warriors. In time, the behavior of many Christians who modeled such values as honesty, faithfulness, and genuine caring began to take effect on the unschooled farmers. As Christianity spread to the northern borders of the empire, it confronted German tribes whose members lived mostly by herding, hunting, and warring with each other. Some of these tribal men joined the Roman army and brought home prestigious Roman wares, often in exchange for German slaves. The Germans became enamored of the luxuries of Roman civilization: its art, architecture, materials, clothing, housing, and the Christian religion embraced by that culture. German kings saw the advantage of one religion to unify the tribes. Often the king or chieftain converted to Christianity accompanied by his whole tribe. Thomas Cahill (1995), a historian, says, "Throughout the Roman World, Christianity had accompanied Romanization. Just as the subject peoples had wanted to become Roman, they came quickly to understand that they wanted to become Christian too (p. 124).

Besides the political and economic advantages, many converts were attracted by the high moral tone of Christianity and the example of many of its adherents who devoted themselves to the poor and needy. Missionaries whom Constantine sent throughout the empire thought they were fulfilling the mandate of Christ, "Go and make disciples of all nations, baptizing them in the name of the Father, Son, and Holy Spirit" (Mt. 20:20). Later bishops sent priests to the outposts, including Patrick to Ireland, Boniface to Germany, and Augustine of Canterbury to England. Inspired by their example and message, thousands of people converted to Christianity. Hans Kung (1995), a theologian, describes some of the attraction of Christianity to the new converts.

> There is no mistaking the fact that Christian monotheism commended itself as a more progressive, enlightened position than polytheism, and that the lofty ethos of Christians, proved superior to that of paganism. Here were clear answers to the problems of guilt and death. Here the Christian religion unlike paganism, appeared grounded in a holy book, the Bible, . . . which sketched out the history of salvation from creation to the end of time. (1995, p. 177)

CONTRIBUTIONS OF MONKS AND NUNS

During the persecutions of the early centuries, the martyrs emerged as the heros and models to be emulated. In the fourth century new heros and models appeared in the forms of monks and nuns, who gave credence to the spirituality and loyalty of the new Christians. They heeded the call of Christ, "If you want to be perfect, go sell what you have, give the money to the poor, and you will have treasure in heaven; then come follow me" (Mt. 19:21). They tried to lead ascetic lives by giving up material comforts, refraining from sexual activity through voluntary celibacy, and living either in community with like-minded individuals or alone in secluded spots to meditate on God.

As the church identified more with the Roman Empire, it began to amass more wealth and prestige. These material and political factors seemed to some to contradict the values of the gospel. In imitation of the first Christian hermits who earlier fled the world and went to live in the Egyptian desert, these monks and nuns longed for a more simple expression of Christianity devoid of personal ownership of property with all its distractions. Wishing to follow the example of the early Christians as portrayed in the Acts of the Apostles, they shared all that they had with each other and the needy.

The monks and nuns lived in independent communities and supported themselves from the livestock, cloth construction, and agriculture of their land held in common. They usually remained close enough to towns and villages to serve the people by teaching them more advanced methods of agriculture, textiles, and animal husbandry. The villagers came to the monastery to hear Mass, to learn methods of healing the sick, and to understand the scriptures that the monks had copied into books.

In the fifth century, Benedict founded the famous monastery of Mount Cassino, which is located south of Rome. Along with poverty, celibacy, and obedience, his monks added the vow of stability, which required them to reside in one monastery all their lives. His rule provided for a balance of work, prayer, and study of scripture. Benedict's sister, Scholastica, founded a monastery for women, where like their brother monks they prayed the scriptures in unison nine times every day. Religious communities following the Benedictine rule spread all over Europe and finally to the New World. Bernard of Clairvaux (1098–1153) was responsible for spreading the monasteries over Europe. Benedictine priests and sisters have erected monasteries in the New World, which graciously bestow hospitality and service to others in the spirit of their founders. The well-known Monks Bread, candies, and jellies help to make them self-supporting like their ancestors.

During the fifth century, the Roman Empire began to endure assaults on its boundaries from the northern tribes. The Roman legions had to withdraw from the areas of Britain and Ireland in order to protect the continent. Eventually, the barbarians triumphed, and western Europe settled into the so called "Dark Ages." Through the efforts of Patrick, the Irish and other residents of the British Isles developed their own Celtic spirituality that found monasticism most attractive. The Irish rural environment with few major towns was most conducive for those trying to strengthen their relationship to God by seclusion and solitude in monasteries. The Irish church organized itself around monasteries headed by an abbot, rather than a bishop who ruled the churches of the larger cites and towns of the empire. The insular position of Ireland protected it from the barbarian invasions that plagued the continent. The Irish monks became responsible for the preservation of Christian scriptures, doctrine, and Roman culture.

Irish monks brought this culture and spirituality back to Europe through the efforts of Columba, who founded the famous monastery of Iona off the coast of Scotland. Iona became noted for the austere lives of the monks, the preservation of knowledge by copying manuscripts, and missionary work in converting the tribes. Columbanus, another Irish monk, sailed to Europe with twelve companions where they preached and built monasteries from northern France to Italy. They made many converts to Christianity and helped to raise the level of civilization of the inhabitants after the Dark Ages by their teaching and example.

The Irish contributed outstanding women to the church also. Briget, along with her Christian mother, was a slave who was sold to an Irish druid. From the druid, Briget learned many secrets of nature, such as healing herbs and special uses of fire and water that could be used to cure illnesses. Briget entered a Christian monastery, where she quickly became abbess. Soon men came to join the abbey and she found herself leading a double monastery at Kildare, one for men and another for women. She founded many monasteries all over Ireland that became centers of learning and service to the surrounding people. They came to learn carpentry, farming, harvesting, weaving, nutrition, and how to care for the sick.

These double monasteries spread to Europe where Hildegard of Bingen, an abbess, had a lasting influence. She instructed the nuns in medicine and midwifery and conducted the first hospitals. Hildegard's nuns developed the art of tapestry and other ornate weavings out of which they constructed beautiful vestments used for liturgical functions. She wrote three theology books as well as books on medicine and science. Her best-known book, which interpreted the nature of the world, is called the *Scivias* or "Know the Ways." Her books became the most important source for knowledge of nature, astronomy, and medicine in the early Middle Ages. Hildegard also authored the first known morality play and composed hymns and liturgical chants for church rituals.

The monks, nuns, and missionaries succeeded in converting the tribes and peoples who inhabited most of the known world of the old Roman Empire. They even reached areas that are no longer Christian today, such as the lands now inhabited by Muslims in North Africa and the Mideast. Christianity had established itself as the acceptable religion for almost everyone in the West by the year 1000.

As the cities grew and the church became more centralized, the monasteries began to be replaced by universities connected to cathedrals as centers of learning.

SIGNIFICANCE OF THE CATHEDRALS

The cathedrals usually were placed in the center of town and were considered the bishop's church. They were the largest buildings in the towns and cities and reflected the people's devotion to God. They were a means of instruction for the unschooled because the walls and stained glass windows portrayed the life of Christ and other scenes from the Bible. Statues of Mary and the other saints brought to reality the presence of those heros and heroines who spent their lives for God. The element of democracy prevailed in the cathedral where the wealthy, rulers, and serfs knelt together before their Creator. The cathedrals belonged to the people who worked together to build them and used them daily for liturgies and frequently for morality plays, art shows, and other cultural and recreational events. Since they were located in the center of town near the markets, the daily visitor could stop to pray and read the news that was attached to the wooden doors. There was even a blue chapel, where lovers would meet when the girl's chaperon would subtly leave so the girl could be visited by her suitor.

These huge and beautiful cathedrals displayed in stone the spirit of medieval Christians whose consciousness of the Divine was ever present. The Gothic form of architecture stressed the spiritual aspirations of the congregation with spires that raised to the skies in praise of God. Modern travelers to Europe can view these impressive buildings from miles away because they dominate the towns and cities.

The cathedrals where they gathered for public worship served as the center of the liturgical life of the Christians. Baptism, the initiation rite of the Christian community, was celebrated sometimes in the church and at other times in a baptistery constructed for that purpose. For example, the famous baptistery in Florence, Italy, near the cathedral is known for the artistry of Ghiberti on its bronze doors. The Christians gathered weekly and often daily in their churches to celebrate the Sacrament of the Eucharist. They believed that the Eucharist, or Mass, reenacted the words and actions of Jesus at the Last Supper. Paul's words in his letter to the Corinthians (1 Cor. 11:23–29) were repeated at each Mass or Liturgy of the Eucharist:

> For I received from the Lord which I also passed on to you, that the Lord Jesus, on the night when he was betrayed, took bread, and when he gave thanks, broke it, and said "This is my Body which is for you. Do this in remembrance of me." In the same way, he also took the cup, saying, "This cup is God's new covenant sealed with my blood. Whenever you drink it, do so in memory of me." For as often as you eat this bread and drink this cup, you proclaim the Lord's death until he comes.

Christians took the words of Christ literally when he identified himself with the bread and wine. They believed that Jesus was present in the bread and the wine and that they were united to Christ and to his presence in each other in the communion service of the Eucharist. A sacrificial element was added to their Catholic perception of the "real presence" of Christ in the Eucharist as they considered the ritual a reenactment of his sacrifice on the cross. They believed that this offering extended over time and space as Christ offered himself anew at each Eucharist or Mass.

At this time seven sacraments were acknowledged by the Church. Baptism and Eucharist were considered sacraments because one encountered the presence of Christ in them. One received the gift of the Spirit in the sacrament of Confirmation. Penitents were reconciled to God and to each other through the sacrament of Penance, now referred to as the Sacrament of Reconciliation. Matrimony united a couple in a graced and permanent relationship, Holy Orders conferred the ministerial priesthood, and Anointing of the Sick completed the sacramental system.

The celebration of holy time included not only prayer and sacraments, but also other calendar feasts assumed aspects of the sacred. Christmas, remembering the Lord's birth, Easter, recalling his resurrection, and Pentecost, the anniversary of the coming of the Holy Spirit, all took on major significance. Feast days of the Blessed Mother and the saints and martyrs became sacred times to celebrate cherished memories.

Some of these revered persons left relics of their person or belongings that believers longed to see. Sacred places that held memories of Jesus, Mary, or the saints became sites of pilgrimage, to which miraculous powers were often attributed. Some pilgrims found themselves healed of physical ailments and left crutches, wheelchairs, and other ornaments at shrines to attest to the miracles. The Holy Land in Palestine held special significance because Christ, God Incarnate, had walked, taught, and performed miracles there. Martyrs were believed to have gone directly to heaven after suffering death for their faith. Tombs of such martyrs as Peter and Paul became sites of pilgrimage where the faithful journeyed to honor their dead, ask forgiveness for sins, or express gratitude for favors received. Large cathedrals as well as local shrines were often built over the tombs of saints and martyrs to house the sacred relics and became sites of pilgrimages, such as St. Peter's Basilica in Rome.

Devotion to Mary, the mother of Jesus, became very popular during the Middle Ages. Devotees found in her a mother figure who would listen to them and bestow her favors upon them. Christians perceived her as an intermediary who would petition Jesus for them.

Remembering his response to his mother at the marriage feast of Cana, where he changed his whole earthly timetable to accommodate her request, they thought he would continue to grant favors to her. Many of the cathedrals of Europe were named after Mary, such as Notre Dame, Our Lady of Chartres, and Santa Maria del Fiore. Famous artists such as Raphael, Cimabue, Giotto, and da Vinci, as well as Michelangelo, have immortalized the Blessed Mother in oil and marble. Modern Christians address Mary with the fifty "Hail Mary" prayers that are counted on beads forming a rosary.

MENDICANTS AND NEW ORDERS OF WOMEN RELIGIOUS

Christianity was also spread by traveling priests and brothers called friars. They left their convents and monasteries to preach the Christian message through word and example. They lived poorly, trying to model their lives on the gospel, and often begged for their food. Some friars were street preachers, attracting large crowds of townspeople who desired to hear the scriptures explained in their own language. Francis of Assisi and Dominic Guzman were founders of two religious orders of friars that were devoted to itinerant preaching and that spread throughout Europe to the New World.

Francis and Clare of Assisi

Francis (d.1226) was the son of a wealthy merchant in the Italian city of Assisi in the twelfth century. He was known to be a fun-loving young man given to entertaining his friends with music and adventure. One day while praying in a dilapidated and abandoned chapel, Francis heard Christ speak to him from a crucifix, telling him to "rebuild my church." Francis took the words literally and began to replenish the abandoned chapels in the area with brick and mortar. Finally, Francis perceived the true meaning of rebuild to mean reform, and he set about to live the simplicity of the gospel. He gave away all his finery and even some of his merchant father's valuable cloths to beggars. He espoused himself to "Lady Poverty," meaning that he would live without material comforts and beg for his food. He preached the message of the gospel to the townsfolk who flocked to hear him. They so admired his zeal and simplicity that many young men began to follow his example. Francis gained 10,000 followers in his lifetime, all dedicated to the spread of the Christian message by word and example. They opened clinics and gave hospitality at their convents to anyone in need. His followers assumed the name of Friars Minor or Lesser Brothers, but usually they are called Franciscans after their founder.

A young woman from the town, whose name was Clare, wanted to follow him, so together they founded a convent for women. Poor, homeless, and sick women were welcomed there to learn about God and express their devotion in prayer. Francis saw his friars spread throughout Europe during his lifetime, and Clare was instrumental in founding many convents for women. Clare's followers are known as Poor Clares and have established monasteries for contemplative prayer all over the world. Other female Franciscans have established hospitals, schools, and colleges all over Europe, Africa, and North and South America. Francis's followers have also founded Franciscan schools and parishes that still adhere to the gospel values of simplicity and poverty.

Dominican Friars and Nuns

Dominic Guzman (d.1221) was a contemporary of Francis and also founded a mendicant order dedicated to active service in the towns and cities. He was a Spanish priest who began as an urban street preacher, where he attracted large crowds who could hear the gospel preached in their own language. He attracted many young men to his way of life, and soon Dominic founded the Order of Preachers popularly called the Dominicans. Realizing the need for orthodox teaching to fight heresy, Dominic sent his preachers to universities where they learned traditional theology and scripture. Dominican scholars addressed the ethical and social needs confronting the newer urban dwellers, which differed somewhat from the concerns of the village and agrarian folk. Dominicans, like Franciscans, traveled over Europe and to the New World, bringing the Christian message by establishing schools and universities. The Dominican nuns and sisters have dedicated themselves to teaching and founding schools and colleges for women. Because Dominic associated with universities, some noted Dominican scholars emanated from them, such as Albert the Great, Thomas Aquinas, and Meister Eckart.

CHRISTIAN THINKERS

Besides reflecting on sacred scripture, Christian scholars began to study faith and doctrine. They began to speculate on the nature of God, the universe, and humans' place in the world. Acknowledging that humans seek happiness as a goal in life, Christian theologians or scholars tried to discover just what makes people happy and how they can attain it. One way to obtain happiness was through knowledge of God, which they thought would strengthen humans' relationship to the Almighty. Theologians taught that if humans better understood their place in God's world, they would be motivated more energetically to attain their present and future happiness. Through the Middle Ages theology was considered to be queen of the sciences, and Christian intellectuals played a great part in the advancement of cultural and intellectual life of its members. The following thinkers contributed greatly to the understanding of Christian doctrine, spirituality, and everyday living.

Augustine (354–430)

Augustine, who lived in the fourth and fifth centuries, tried to explain the problem of evil that plagues all religious believers. It is difficult to understand how a good God can allow evil to exist in the world. Augustine said that there were two realms of existence, one that he called the City of God and the other, the City of Man. In the City of God, the faithful are loyal to God's will and live according to divine precepts. They experience joy and happiness in knowing that their interests lie in union with the concerns of heaven. Those inhabiting the City of Man live in selfishness and sin and experience the unhappiness that results from the situations that they choose. This earthly existence is temporary as are their impermanent pleasures. Augustine suggests that one must give up attachments to earthly things in order to savor the happiness of the spiritual, which is the true gift of God.

Augustine also tried to explain the trinity in terms of one Godhead or divine essence that was common to all three persons, the Father, Son and Holy Spirit. The persons share one nature internally but differ only in their external relationships. Theologian Hans Kung gives his interpretation of Augustine's theory:

> Augustine constructs the Trinity as God's unfolding of God's self . . . The Son is "begotten". . . in the divine act of thinking from the substance of the Father: he is the Father's personal word and image. The Spirit "proceeds" from the Father (the one who loves) and the Son (the one who is loved) . . . so the Spirit is the personified love between Father and Son. The trinity clearly expresses not only the unity of the one divine nature, but also the interrelationship of the three persons. (1985, pp. 300–301)

New ideas that challenged traditional thinking about faith and God reached Europe in the thirteenth century. The crusaders returned from the Byzantine Empire with writings from the early church fathers that the western Empire had not seen before. They brought with them some of the writings from pagan antiquity, including the philosophy of Aristotle. Their encounter with the Muslims brought new understandings of mathematics and architecture. These new streams of thought could reach more scholars because the universities were replacing the monasteries as centers of learning. Bishops had established schools that were associated with their churches and appropriately called them cathedral schools. The traditional liberal arts of logic, rhetoric, grammar, arithmetic, geometry, astronomy, and music constituted most of the curriculum. Some of the more outstanding cathedral schools gradually grew into universities where scholars congregated to study theology.

The new Christian theological scholars used a method of inquiry called scholasticism in order to learn more about God and their world. They would critically reflect on their faith, using scripture, writings of the early Christian witnesses, and the thinking of theologians and philosophers. These new scholars believed that they did not have to depend only on scripture and the works of the past but could use their own reasoning ability to understand God and the supernatural. They thought that human happiness would be enhanced by a greater knowledge of the nature and love of God. This knowledge would lead to a greater appreciation of the graced existence that had been given to humanity. Scholars thought that use of human reason, which would lead to a greater understanding of the things of God, would improve the faith of Christians and thus increase their relationship with God.

Anselem, Archbishop of Canterbury (ca. 1033–1109)

Anselem was considered the father of scholasticism because of his use of logic and original thinking in trying to explain the truths of faith. His starting point was faith in God and the truths of sacred scripture. He then applied the scholastic method of inquiry and reflection to better understand these truths. His atonement theory as an explanation of the incarnation and death of Jesus is still popular in many Christian churches today. He noticed in his feudal society that the king, lords, and vassals had more prestige and power than the serfs and peasants. If a lower-class peasant offended a higher-class lord or king, his punishment was greater than an offense against another peasant because the honor of the upper-class nobles was greater than that of the lower classes. Honor was esteemed in feudal society because it included a person's estate, titles, lands, and status, so an offense against honor became an offense against the whole social order. Anselem applied this situation to an offense against God, whose honor is so great that no human being was worthy to atone or make reparation for it. Only a person equal to God could atone or repair for such a heinous crime. Therefore, God had to become human in the person of

Jesus in the incarnation and to suffer death on the cross to redeem humankind by atoning for their sin.

Anselem coined the phrase, "I believe in order to understand." Motivated by faith in God, Anselem used his intellect to gain a greater knowledge and understanding of the goodness of God. Utilizing the tools of philosophy, he could create a theology that was credible to the scholars and ordinary believers of his day. His definition of theology, "faith seeking understanding," is as meaningful to theologians today as it was to Anselem.

Thomas Aquinas (1225–1274)

Thomas joined the new Order of Preachers founded by Dominic, because he was attracted to their concept of poverty and love of learning. He prepared a *summa,* or compendium of Christian doctrine, in which he tried to harmonize faith with philosophy and reason. He believed that natural reason provides information about the world and humankind that can ultimately lead to knowledge of God. One can deduce truths about the supernatural, invisible world from what is known in the natural, visible world. For example, when reflecting on the orderly design in nature, one notices that seasons follow each other sequentially; fruit trees bear fruit, not vegetables; species reproduce their own kind; and so on. From such natural observations, one can deduce that there must be a Divine Designer or Supernatural Intelligence that provides humans with such stable and providential care.

Although reason guided by faith can enable one to understand some natural truths concerning God, Thomas believed that there are some supernatural truths that must be based on faith alone. For example, reason might be able to discern that God really exists, but only faith could penetrate the knowledge that God is Triune. Revelation that comes from God, as in scripture, cannot be reasoned away, but philosophical tools such as logic can be used to further one's understanding of the sacred. Thomas recognized human intellectual ability and at the same time respected the goodness of God who reveals truths necessary for salvation. For this accomplishment, he was given the title "Doctor of the Church" in the sixteenth century.

Bonaventure (1217–1274)

Like Augustine, Bonaventure realized that one's response to God required more than just the intellect. Emotions and experience are equally valuable as one aspires not only to know God but to embrace God in love. True to his Franciscan heritage, Bonaventure appreciated all of creation as revealing God's glory and concern for humans. However, it was humans who most closely imaged God because only humans, of all creation, possessed emotions and intellect, which enables them to love as God loves.

Bonaventure claimed that the best knowledge of God could be attained through contemplative prayer, by which one can directly experience the love of God. Knowledge secured by the direct experience of God is superior to any knowledge obtained by logical reasoning because God chooses to give it to the seeker. Experiential knowledge of love is so personal and unique that it cannot be taught in a classroom in the same manner as philosophical knowledge. However, Bonaventure did not disdain the use of reason and philosophy to investigate theological truths that lead to knowledge of God. Direct experience

> is also. . . a philosophy. . . in the same sense that Socrates used the term—a reasoned manner of living, which has at its aim the pursuit of wisdom, a process of purification which frees the soul to follow the natural tendency towards goodness and truth. (Herr, 1985, p. 73)

The ideas of Bonaventure regarding the great diversity found in nature can be applied to modern times. He said that the many forms found in plants, animals, and humans were necessary to reflect the many aspects of the perfection of God. No singular creature or species of plant or animal could adequately reflect the totality of God's perfection, so every one is necessary to manifest the different aspects of God in the uniqueness of their own existence.

SUMMARY

As Christianity spread, church authorities found it necessary to have a unified approach to the declaration of doctrine. Early church councils were held to define beliefs in God, Christ, the Holy Spirit and the place of Mary. Attraction to Roman civilization and culture helped to spread Christianity to the outlying tribes of Europe. The high moral tone of the Christians accompanied by the zeal of the missionaries contributed to the rapid rate of converts to the new religion. Monks and nuns taught by their example as well as their words how to transmit the gospel message. Benedict, Columba, Columbanus, Scholastica, Briget, and Hildegard left their mark on civilization as a result of their dedication to God and service to others.

The cathedrals of the Middle Ages still remain as images to the faith of their builders. Visitors to these beautiful sites can still experience the rich liturgical life that was so important to the original Christian participants. The Liturgy of the Mass, or the Eucharist, is said daily in these outstanding edifices. Sacraments are celebrated in their churches and Christians approach God through private and congregational prayer. Some of these cathedrals still draw pilgrims who desire to see relics from saints or walk on the same ground that Jesus did.

Mendicant orders of priests and sisters desired to follow the gospel portrayal of Jesus more closely by becoming itinerant preachers, teachers, and healers. Disciples of Francis and Clare have promoted the Franciscan ideals all over the world. Dominican preachers have established schools of higher learning where Christian faith can be transmitted to students of all ages.

Students and teachers began to gravitate to universities where such luminaries as Anselem, Thomas Aquinas, and Bonaventure proclaimed the use of reason and one's own intelligence to fathom the goodness of God.

DISCUSSION QUESTIONS

1. Why were converts attracted to Christianity? Would some of these factors attract converts today?
2. Why was it important for the church leaders to meet at the councils of Nicea, Ephesus, and Chalcedon? Can you think of any reasons to call a council at the present time?
3. What is the importance of the monks and nuns? Might you ever try to visit a monastery? What would you expect to find there?
4. How do the medieval cathedrals differ from modern churches? Why can one call those cathedrals the poor man's bible? What types of buildings dominate modern cities, and what is their significance?
5. How did the sacraments contribute to the spiritual life of medieval Christians? Do the sacraments have the same effect in the lives of contemporary Christians?
6. How did the mendicants influence the spread of Christianity?
7. How did the rise of universities influence theology?
8. Which one of the Christian thinkers mentioned in the text speaks most clearly to you?
9. Does faith precede knowledge or does knowledge precede faith?

WORKS CITED

Cahill, Thomas. *How the Irish Saved Civilization.* New York: Doubleday, 1995.

Herr, William. *Great Catholic Thinkers.* Chicago: Thomas Moore Press, 1985.

Kung, Hans. *Great Christian Thinkers.* New York: Continuum, 1985.

Kung, Hans. *Christianity.* New York: Continuum, 1995.

Chapter Six

Divisions within Christendom

EARLIER SEPARATIONS OF THE EAST

Christianity in the Eastern Empire spread from the area around Byzantium, which Constantine renamed Constantinople, to the Slavs of Eastern Europe and Russia through the efforts of two missionary brothers, Cyril and Methodius. They translated the Bible and liturgical books into local Slavonic languages so the people could hear the gospel preached and the rituals celebrated in their own language. The Eastern church is called Orthodox because the members believe they are loyal to the original tradition of Christianity. Adherents of the Orthodox tradition perceive themselves as the true believers, not only in the teachings of the Bible, but also but also in the writings of the church fathers. There are 160 million members of the Orthodox Church who number second only to Roman Catholics in Christian denominations. Like Roman Catholics, the Orthodox believe in the necessity of tradition to interpret the scriptures and their adaptation to changing cultural times.

A conflict developed in the eleventh century between the Eastern and the Latin or Western churches over the word in the Nicene Creed *Filioque,* which is translated "and the Son." The original Nicene Creed depicted the Spirit as coming from the Father. The later addition of Filioque by the Western church said that the Holy Spirit proceeded from the Father and the Son, which indicated a subordinate position of the Spirit. The West kept Filioque in their version of the Nicene Creed, while the East rejected the addition. In order to keep peace between the Latin Western Empire and the Byzantine East, the Pope urged the use of the Apostles' Creed to replace the Nicene Creed in liturgical functions.

Another rift occurred in the eleventh century when the Latin church insisted that the Eastern churches located in Italy conform to the use of Latin in their rituals. The Patriarch of Constantinople retaliated by insisting that Western churches in Constantinople adopt Greek customs. The rift became unamenable when the Patriarch closed the Latin churches when they refused to conform to Greek liturgies and language. A schism or separation followed in 1054 that divided Christianity into the Latin Roman Catholic West of Europe and the Orthodox Catholic East of the Balkans, Greece, and Russia. Because of the close ties of the Eastern church to national politics, many Orthodox churches assume the names of their countries, such as Serbian Orthodox, Greek Orthodox, or Russian Orthodox.

RIGHT BELIEFS AND PRACTICES

The Orthodox Church adopted the same seven sacraments of the Roman Catholic Church, with some small accommodations. Infants are confirmed at Baptism and become eligible to receive Holy Communion as full members of the church. The liturgy is celebrated in a rich, dramatic matter, accompanied by incense and choral singing without musical instruments. Orthodox believers feel that the liturgy helps them to accomplish their goal in life to become more spiritual. Because humans are created in the image (icon) of God, that image should not become tarnished by sin. The image of God should grow and develop until humans become more divine by resembling the Spirit of God within them. The Orthodox, along with Roman Catholics, see the need of tradition to interpret the scriptures rather than relying on individual understandings. They accept the first seven of the twenty-one ecumenical councils of the church, most of which occurred before the separation.

The Orthodox Church allows priests to marry before ordination, but bishops must remain celibate. Bishops were often chosen from among the monks whose monasteries are dotted throughout the East. Monasticism in the East seemed to have a different purpose from that of the West, where monasteries were centers of learning. Orthodox monks devote themselves to prayer and contemplation, in which they seek union with God in the mystical experience. Some of the more famous monasteries, such as Mount Athos in Greece, attract visitors today. Many go as tourists, but others go as pilgrims to visit a holy spot where they can experience the presence of God.

Much of the Byzantine art has been preserved in icons (or flat pictures of Christ, Mary, and the saints). Some of these have been imbedded in beautiful mosaics, which can be seen in the famous churches of Constantinople (modern Istanbul) and Ravenna, Italy. Icons are usually painted on wood with a gold background signifying heaven. They are considered not only objects of art but also images of special devotion. A row of icons separates the sanctuary from the congregation, which enables the people to experience the coming down to earth of Jesus and the saints during the liturgy. Orthodox churches are usually very colorful, having onion-shaped domes crowned with golden crosses.

The Orthodox Church was more closely tied to the secular rulers than the Western church, where the Pope exercised strong central authority. The highest ranking prelate, the Patriarch of Constantinople, saw himself so closely tied to the emperor that the secular ruler could approve or disapprove of his clerical appointments. The church was protected and financed by the secular rulers, who sometimes interfered in spiritual matters. Rather than giving allegiance to the central authority of the Pope, Orthodox Catholics experience a more decentralized form of authority. The Patriarch of Istanbul is considered the titular head of the church, but authority rests with fifteen other patriarchs of autonomous churches, mostly of different national origins.

The political alliance between church and state became most prominent when the tzar (or emperor) of Russia perceived himself as a protector of the church, its secular minister, similar to the Byzantine emperors of old. The church and state became so allied that when the communist revolution overthrew the monarchial government, the church was vanquished also. In recent years, the Russian Orthodox Church that was forced underground during the communist era has re-emerged to become a vibrant spiritual entity ministering to the needs of the Russian people.

Recent popes have made some attempts at reunion between the Orthodox and Roman Catholic churches. The governmental structure of decentralization of authority to many patriarchs has made it difficult for the Eastern Orthodox to accept the authority of only one bishop (the bishop of Rome, known as the Pope). The strong ties to a national government hinders allegiance to the universal structure of the Roman Catholic Church. But serious efforts have been made by both Catholic groups to promote harmony that is consistent with the gospel.

CONDITIONS LEADING TO THE DISSOLUTION OF THE UNION OF CHURCH AND SOCIETY

Historians and sociologists of religion still profess amazement at the phenomenon of the Middle Ages called Christendom. The political, social, economic, and spiritual aspects of society seemed to meld into one, with the magnificent cathedrals standing as witness to this union.

The spiritual seemed to predominate, with the hierarchial structures of the church and the secular structures of society working together to maintain this unity of Christendom. Feudalism, with so many of its lands owned by the church, controlled the economic life of the peasants and lords. Most schools and universities were tied to the church, and even the art, music, and other cultural aspects of civilization depicted religious motifs. The frequent plagues that ravaged the population instilled an awareness of death that compelled the faithful to look beyond this life to eternity. Prayer and pilgrimages were powerful means to atone for one's sins and prepare one for heaven.

The fifteenth and sixteenth centuries ushered in significant political, social, and economic changes. Politically, a spirit of nationalism emerged in many areas where the local princes preferred the use of the vernacular over Latin in their schools, businesses, and political endeavors. The political leaders of smaller states longed for independence from the Pope and Roman emperor and began to find opportunities to execute their autonomy. A new class of bankers and merchants in the cities strengthened a money economy that was replacing the feudal economy of the rural areas. The rise of a middle class that founded its own schools and universities gave impetus to a love of learning of secular subjects. Even the arts took on a more secular nature, depicting an appreciation of nature and the human body.

The church was not exempt from the changing societal conditions. Warfare had weakened the church economically, and the laxity and secular preferences of some of the popes had lessened the respect of the laity for papal leadership. Some of the church leaders seemed more interested in institutional maintenance with its pomp and glory than in the pastoral needs of the people. Reform was needed to return to the simplicity and spirituality of the early church. The mendicants had achieved some reform within the church by living and preaching the gospel message of service to the people. The next group of reformers dissipated the monolithic entity of church and state.

PROTESTANT REFORMATION IN THE WEST

Protestant reform destroyed the medieval ideal of a united Christendom where disputes could be settled by church hierarchies and councils. Protestant teachings stressed the importance of the individual who could approach God directly, lessening the importance of church intermediaries. After the reformation, the secular or national state exercised its authority over the lives of the people, which divested the papacy of much of its authority and power.

The Protestant Reformation caused the Catholic Church to examine more closely some of the issues that caused dissention among the believers. Because the reformers protested some of the beliefs and practices of the Catholic Church, they were called Protestants. The four main forms of protestant Christianity were led by Martin Luther (Lutherans), John Calvin (Reformed), the English Church (Anglican), and the Anabaptists (or radicals). Most of the issues concerning the reformers centered on church authority, the sacraments, and notions of salvation.

Martin Luther (1483–1546)

Martin Luther distinguished himself as a scholar when he was an Augustinian monk. He taught theology and scripture at the University of Wittenberg in northern Germany. Luther felt overwhelmed at his own unworthiness before the majesty of God. He tried to make up for his self-perceived sinfulness by performing such penances as fasting, long prayers, and sleep deprivation. He found no satisfaction from these practices until one day he happened upon a phrase from the letter of Paul to the Romans. "The saving justice of God: a justice based upon faith, . . . As it says in the scripture: anyone who is upright through faith will live" (Rom. 1:17). Meditating on this reassuring phrase, Luther derived his teaching on justification by faith over good works. Because he found such satisfaction from scripture, he began to focus more on its message. Luther began to question the need of church tradition to interpret scripture, because he saw the Bible as the source of God's revelation in place of the teachings of the church. His emphasis on scripture led him to translate the Bible into his native German, thus enabling more of the faithful to read and understand it.

The crisis that precipitated the break with the Catholic Church had to do with the practice of granting indulgences. In the beginning, Luther was not opposed to the use of indulgences, which drew on the treasury of merit secured by the death of Jesus and the saints. This merit would not forgive sins but would do away with the punishment due to sin that would be experienced in this world or the next. Many other religions, such as Hinduism and Buddhism, have merit-producing activities that reduce bad karma, increasing the chance of ceasing the endless round of rebirths. Pope Urban in the eleventh century granted indulgences to all who enlisted in the first crusade, which was to make safe the places of pilgrimage in the Holy Land.

However, the practice moved to a new level when these indulgences appeared to be sold. Many Christians were making pilgrimages to Rome in order to gain indulgences. Johan Tetzel, a Dominican friar, went to Luther's area of Saxony in Germany and told the people that if they would give him the money that they would have spent if they went on a pilgrimage to Rome, he would give them an indulgence. The people were satisfied because they would not have to leave their farms, cattle, and families. Tetzel was happy because he could send money to Rome for the rebuilding of Constantine's church, erected over the grave of St. Peter. Luther was not happy because he thought that the selling of indulgences violated principles of Catholic teaching. He appealed to his German prince to force Tetzel out of the province. Frederick of Saxony was most willing to accommodate Luther, because he kept in his castle church thousands of relics, which he charged the faithful to view. He saw Tetzel as offering competition to his own money-making enterprise.

Luther was so upset over the perversion of church teaching regarding indulgences that he nailed 95 theses or arguments to the door of the castle church at Wittenberg. Conflicting groups gathered on both sides of the issue, but rising German nationalism weighted the arguments in favor of rejecting the outside interference of the Pope and emperor. Other frustrated Catholics who felt overburdened by taxation clamored against the exploitation placed on them by corrupt church officials. Pope Leo X asked Luther to recant his positions and his attack on the church. Luther refused and was excommunicated from the church. When Luther was called before the secular court at the Diet of Worms in 1521, he again refused to deny his teachings. He found himself in the uncomfortable position of defying both the Pope and the emperor of the Holy Roman Empire.

Luther married an ex-nun, Katerina Von Bora, and together they raised a large family. Their home became a meeting place for scholars who discussed, among other things, Luther's teaching on justification by faith and the use of scripture rather than the teachings of church as the authority for Christian living. He accepted only two sacraments from the Catholic church, Baptism and Holy Eucharist. Because he objected to the separation between the clerics and the laity, he advocated the "priesthood of the faithful," in which everyone could communicate directly with God, without a mediator. Protestant clergy, who are allowed to marry, usually adopt the title of pastor or minister, because the title of priest indicates a mediator between the people and God. Luther is considered by most scholars of religion as the originator of the Protestant Reformation, although he claimed that he did not intend to start a new church. His followers are called Lutherans and number among the most prominent Protestant denominations.

John Calvin (1509–1569)

John Calvin agreed with Luther that humans are unable to achieve salvation by such works as prayers, pilgrimages, veneration of saints and their relics, receiving the sacraments, and charitable actions. He believed that humans are justified by faith alone, but he carried the power of God to its logical conclusion in his doctrine of election or predestination. Calvin made it clear that some individuals are called by God to be saved and others are called to be damned. Only God has the power to save or damn someone; neither personal choice nor certain actions on the part of individuals can determine their fate. One can somewhat surmise one's destiny if one acts in a godly fashion, trying to follow God's revelation as found in the scriptures. Although the doctrine of predestination sounds somewhat strange to moderns, it was supposed to reduce the anxiety of Christians regarding their salvation. Instead of working hard at penances, pilgrimages, and good works, they should leave their salvation up to God.

Calvin, like Luther, accepted the two sacraments of Baptism and Communion, which he called "The Lord's Supper." The reformation churches replaced the hierarchal authority of the Catholic Church with the priesthood of the faithful and the authority of the Bible. Calvin devised a church-based system of government in Geneva, Switzerland, employing small representative bodies of laypeople and church elders to govern the people. This system, which is now called Presbyterian, is more democratic than the hierarchal organization of the Catholic Church. However, it could also be oppressive because the religious laws in the city forbade dancing, restricted public speech, and even regulated the names given to infants at Baptism. Those who did not live up to the strict moral laws could be excommunicated. In its extreme form, even the clothing of the members was regulated in Holland and by the English Puritans. (Remember *The Scarlet Letter* in Puritan American literature?) Rembrandt's paintings of the black, high-collared suits and hats on the men and the very modest clothing of the women represent some of the regulations and stern customs of the Reformed or Calvinist communities.

Calvin's ethical system has been linked to the rise of capitalism by Max Weber, a sociologist of religion. Calvin advocated hard work and self-denial, with little time spent in frivolous recreation. His desire to imitate the worshipping community of the early church led to great simplicity in his church buildings. Calvin saw no need for murals or stained glass windows depicting the life of Christ, because everyone should be able to read the Bible. He even banned instrumental music to accompany the hymns at church services because the Acts of the Apostles did not mention them. The church rituals centered on Bible readings and sermons with little other ceremony. As a result, there was no call to spend money on large, beautifully decorated churches, nor on any recreational activities on the part of the people. Since church members were directed to work hard and save their money, the most attractive outlet for their surplus was to reinvest their capital in new ventures.

When John Knox spread the Calvinist Reformed Church to Scotland, it took the name Presbyterian because of its more democratic government, ruled by presbyters from the local churches. Without government interference under the laissez-faire policy, capitalism was able to grow. The Reformed Church spread to Holland and northern Germany, where the commerce of the Hanseatic League promoted more development of capitalism. Weber suggests that the form of the Reformed Church that spread to the Puritans in England influenced America's own form of capitalism. Ben Franklin, although he was a Deist, reflected the Reformed tradition's emphasis on hard work and frugal living. Sayings have been attributed to him, such as "A penny saved is a penny earned," "Idle hands are the Devil's workshop," and "A bird in the hand is worth two in the bush."

Calvin wrote the "Institutes of the Christian Religion," which formed the theology of the reformed churches and the denominations derived from his church in Geneva. Congregationalist churches, Puritans, Presbyterians, Dutch Reformed, and even part of the Baptist Church base much of their theology on his teachings.

The English Reform (1534)

The English reform, like the Lutheran and Calvin reforms, centered on objections to the authority of the Roman Catholic Church. Yet there were very few doctrinal disagreements in England over scripture, justification by faith, or divine election. Henry VIII, a Tudor king, sought an annulment from his marriage to his brother's widow, Catherine of Aragon. The Pope refused to grant it because he did not think there were adequate grounds. Henry wanted a male heir to insure the succession of Tudor kings, but Catherine only provided him with a daughter, Mary. Henry had become enamored of Anne Boleyn, who was pregnant by him. To rid himself of Catherine, Henry placed the church under control of the Crown. Then he could give himself the desired annulment. Anne delivered a daughter, called Elizabeth. Still desiring a son, Henry had Anne beheaded and married one of her ladies in waiting, Jane, who provided him with a son, Edward.

Edward VI was a sickly child who did not live until adulthood, but at nine years of age, he succeeded Henry at his death. Henry's subsequent marriages had not produced any children, so the throne of England was kept in the Tudor family through Edward, Mary, and Elizabeth, whose long reign transformed England into an international power.

Henry consolidated his position as head of the church by dissolving the monasteries, convents, and sites of pilgrimage and selling their lands to fill the national treasury. He then created a national church called Anglican, which was politically and financially secure. When Edward died as a teenager, Mary, the daughter of Catherine and Henry, became queen. She tried to return England to Roman Catholicism, but she died in 1558, after only five years in power. She was succeeded by Elizabeth, whose long reign really established the Church of England. Elizabeth tried to find a middle ground between the Catholic and Protestant elements so as to satisfy them both. Her efforts appear in the *Book of Common Prayer,* in which the Catholic view of the Real Presence in the Eucharist and the Protestant stance of the bread and wine as a memorial of Christ's death are both represented. Cranmer, Henry's archbishop of Canterbury, had introduced the Bible in the English language. The King James version, which has been so popular in English-speaking countries, succeeded this edition in 1611. Much of the structure and rituals of the Roman Catholic Church remained, but some elements, like the veneration of saints, were removed.

Still, Anglicanism as the Church of England remains the most conservative branch of the reformed tradition because of its similarity to Roman Catholicism. Some groups, such as the Puritans, wanted to purify the Anglican Church from the Roman elements. Their protests, which led to their persecution, resulted in their journey to the New World to practice their religion freely. The Congregational, Methodist, and some Baptist churches are also derived from the Anglican Church. The reigning monarch of Great Britain is still considered the head of the Church of England, aided by the archbishop of Canterbury. Some attempts at reunion with the Roman Catholic Church have been made by modern popes, but no definite movement toward union has emerged.

The Radical Reformers: Anabaptist (1527) and Others

To the Radicals, the Reformed tradition still had too much authority vested in their pastors, and ties to the state were still too strong. The Radicals believed that membership in the church should be voluntary; consequently they objected to the state-imposed regulation that all infants should be baptized. The term Anabaptists means "rebaptizers," representing the thinking of the Radicals that only adults, after a profession of faith, should be baptized. In their desire to follow only the scriptures, the Anabaptists became pacifists and objected to religious wars. They also imitated the early Christian practice of sharing all things in common, which is the mark of community living. Their strong separation from the state compelled them to hold no public office nor make appeals to state authorities to settle disputes.

They tried to model their idea of Christian perfection on the early Christian community of the New Testament. Anabaptists refrain from profanity, lying, strife, and intemperate eating and drinking. They observe simplicity in dress and home furnishings and allow no distinction between clergy and laity. They expelled community members who did not adhere to the community beliefs and practices. The community adopted Calvin's ideas on divine election, whereby God knows who is saved and who is damned. One could be certain to be part of God's elect if one made a conscious, free act of believing in adult baptism and then persevered in the commitment. Those who did not make such a commitment were outside their group and had to suffer the insecurity of not really knowing if they would be saved.

Some of the Protestant groups derived from the Anabaptists see themselves as separated from the world whose secular values they reject. The Mennonites prefer the simplicity of communal living, the Quakers refuse to participate in any form of violence, and the Amish refuse to use electricity and machines that were invented after their establishment as a religious congregation. The Anabaptists have bestowed a legacy of democracy upon their followers, in which decisions are made in common rather than by the clergy. Congregations choose their own pastors and adopt and enforce their own rules, much in the same way that modern Pentecostal and Holiness churches do.

Roman Catholic Reform

By the 1530s all of Scandinavia, Scotland, England, and much of France, Austria, and Germany had severed ties with the Roman Catholic Church. A council was called in Trent, Italy, in 1545 to define Catholic views on grace and faith, the issue that gave such impetus to Luther's and Calvin's reforms. The council fathers followed a middle course between saying that salvation depends upon God (grace) or that everything depends upon human effort. They claimed that salvation does come from God as pure gift, but that it requires some measure of human cooperation. In response to the Protestant teaching that scripture is the sole source of authority, the council insisted that the teaching magisterium of the church (councils, unwritten traditions, rulings of the popes) along with scripture were to be the authority for faith and teaching. The council upheld the number of sacraments at seven and tried to heal the abuses instigated by the church hierarchy. Indulgences could not be sold, celibacy was enforced, and bishops were to take more responsibility for their dioceses by overseeing the finances and the moral and spiritual discipline of the faithful. By reforming itself from within, the Roman Catholic Church hoped to remove the grounds for Protestant criticisms.

The council fathers thought it necessary to define precisely the Catholic Church teachings so that everyone would clearly understand its differences from Protestantism. Ignatius of Loyola, the founder of the Jesuit order of priests, seemed dedicated to this task. The Jesuits were a new religious order swearing service to the Pope through education and missionary work. They founded schools to educate the faithful from primary level through university. They were dedicated to the theological education of priests and established seminaries to fulfill this purpose.

New orders of women were established, such as the Daughters of Charity, who founded clinics and hospitals. The Ursulines dedicated themselves to the education of women and girls by establishing schools in Europe and the New World. Other Catholic women religious left the confines of their monasteries to bring the message of Christ to the poor and marginal of society. While the theologians were defining church teachings, other Catholics were investigating the devotional and spiritual dimension of religion. Teresa of Avila (1515–82), a Carmelite nun, wrote about her mystical or direct experience of God. John of the Cross (1542–91), a Carmelite priest, spoke of humans' desire for perfection that could be reached by an intimate relationship with God. Ignatius of Loyola wrote the *Spiritual Exercises* in 1523, a four-week program of prayer and meditation, with the purpose of deepening the relation of the Christian to Christ. The church saw the need to embrace the whole of human personality—the intellect, by making its teachings credible; the emotions, by its devotions and mystical tendencies; and the will, by motivating one to commit to faith.

The council upheld the practice of veneration of saints. The faithful believed that they could ask the saints, who they perceived as abiding in heaven, to intercede for them to Christ. Special power was attributed to Mary, the mother of Jesus, whom the faithful honored with rosary prayer and processions. Medieval art glorified Mary with beautiful and elaborate mosaics, paintings, and statues of her, usually holding the infant Jesus. Famous museums are filled with paintings of the Madonna and child by such renowned artists as Raphael, da Vinci, and Murillo. Michelangelo's delicate Pieta statue of Mary holding the dead body of Jesus is considered one of the world's most beautiful pieces of art. Mary counted both men and women among her devotees but gave especially to women a model of dignity to which they could aspire. Shrines and churches have been erected in memory of her appearances or apparitions. The shrine at Lourdes, France, has gained international prominence for the many medically documented cures that have occurred at the miraculous spring. Catholics from all over the world visit shrines in Fatima, Portugal, and Mexico City to gain favors and give glory to their Blessed Mother.

Protestants, who dethroned Mary and other female saints and closed the monasteries for women, effected a change in the status of women. The nuns in the monasteries exerted some leadership in the church and its service to others, but Protestantism restricted women to the home as wives and mothers. Martin Luther (1958) said, "She sits at home. . . . Just as the snail carries its house with it, so the wife should stay at home and look after the affairs of the household. . . ." (p. 203). John Calvin resurrected the biblical laws that said an adulterous wife should be stoned to death, although the unfaithful husband should not be punished. Later Protestant groups, such as the Quakers and Shakers, treated women more equally. Modern members of Protestant and Catholic denominations recognize and affirm women for positions of leadership in their churches and in society.

INFLUENCE OF THE ENLIGHTENMENT AND RENAISSANCE

The Enlightenment, with roots that can be traced back to the Renaissance of the fifteenth and sixteenth centuries, was an intellectual and cultural movement during the seventeenth and eighteenth centuries that emphasized the authority of human reasoning ability over the authority of revelation of scripture or church doctrine. Alister McGrath distinguishes between reason and rationalism, which he attributes to the Enlightenment. He claims that reason is the basic human faculty of thinking, based on argument and evidence. "It is theologically neutral and poses no threat to faith—unless it is regarded as the only source of knowledge about God. It then becomes rationalism, which is the exclusive reliance on reason alone, and a refusal to allow any weight to be given to divine revelation (p. 178).

Divine revelation refers to scripture that Christians believed was revealed by God. The church had interpreted the revelation of scripture for believers for centuries. Now, humans realized that by using their own intellect, they were able to interpret those scriptures without appealing to the authority of the church. Great advances had been made in science because such individuals as Galileo advocated scientific study rather than relying on theology for answers to questions regarding nature. The Enlightenment challenged believers to look beyond the Bible for explanations of natural phenomena. It was a shock to some that the earth was not the center of the universe, as the biblical writers had indicated. This new knowledge led to further investigation on the part of scholars, artists, and scientists.

The Renaissance brought changes in most areas of human life.

The agricultural and rural atmosphere of the medieval world appeared more conducive to communal living, where dependence upon God and other humans seemed necessary. Cities and towns were more likely to stimulate the growth of individualism because trades and commerce demanded less communal effort for success. Emphasis changed from dependence upon God to dependence upon human effort to insure one's livelihood. The emphasis on human effort gave impetus to advances in art, literature, and science. Leonardo da Vinci, Michelangelo, and other artists made use of perspective, which made their work appear more realistic. Mapmakers were no longer bound by pilgrimage routes but produced more accurate maps that enabled travel to the East and the New World. The Renaissance traveler used knowledge of geography for commercial opportunities rather than pilgrimages to sacred spots that honored God.

Even the popes became great patrons of the arts that marked the Renaissance. They collected many works of famous artists, making the Vatican museum the largest in the West. Pope Sixtus IV commissioned Michelangelo to paint the Sistine chapel and to design much of the new St. Peter's Basilica. Individuals became famous, such as the artists da Vinci and Raphael, the explorers Da Gama and Columbus, scientist Isaac Newton, and philosophers Descartes and Voltaire.

The emphasis on theology in education expanded to include the study of literature, Greek, philosophy, mathematics, and science. Students were taught to question traditional beliefs and to use their intellect to come to reasonable conclusions. But when it came to questioning the revelation of God through scripture or the teachings of the church, a dilemma resulted: Is religious belief rational, or can religious beliefs be subjected to human reason? Moderns might not find such questions shocking, but to a religion and a civilization that based its authority, rituals, morality, practices, and theology for many centuries on the revelation of God through scripture and church tradition, the question was very threatening. If humans were capable of understanding God and nature using their reasoning ability alone, was there a need for an institutional church?

The Christian scholars reacted to the challenge by trying to prove that Christianity was a reasonable religion. They found ways that reason supported key points of revelation rather than only contradicting it. John Locke's book, *The Reasonableness of Christianity* (1695), tried to prove rationally the events of the New Testament such as the divinity of Jesus and the historicity of his miracles. Even Voltaire (1694–1778) who attacked the clericalism of the Catholic Church, wrote of the importance of religion in human life because of its emphasis on morality and constructive human relations. The Enlightenment both supported Christianity and forced it to evolve in new directions. The next chapter will show some of these new directions as Christianity found a home in the New World.

SUMMARY

The medieval phenomenon of the monolithic entity of church and state began to dissipate with the separation of the Eastern Orthodox and Roman Catholic churches in the eleventh century. Both churches keep similar traditions, scriptures, and sacraments but differ in their political arrangements with their national origins. Only the Roman Catholics claim allegiance to the Pope while the Eastern Orthodox place their authority in a group of national patriarchs.

Changes in society and in the church were among the causes for the Protestant Reform. Such men as Martin Luther, John Calvin, and Henry VIII of England directly influenced the beginnings of Protestantism. Followers of the Anabaptist movements have contributed to ideals of pacifism, egalitarianism, and communal living.

The Catholic hierarchy recognized the need for reform and called the Council of Trent to define some beliefs and practices that were being questioned. New religious orders, such as the Jesuits, arose to teach the doctrines of the Catholic reform. Active orders of women religious established grammar and high schools as well as colleges for women to promote and define Catholic doctrine. The Daughters of Charity built and staffed hospitals and clinics, trying to put into practice the gospel message of charity.

The Enlightenment presented challenges to Christianity because of its emphasis on the use of reason for explanations of phenomena that were previously explained by divine revelation. If humans' natural reasoning ability seemed superior for the purpose of understanding to that of the Bible and church tradition, was there a need for institutional churches? Renaissance artists, scientists, educators, and philosophers did not give up on the existence of God but expanded to secular subjects and new directions.

DISCUSSION QUESTIONS

1. How do the Roman and Eastern Orthodox Catholics differ in their beliefs and practices?
2. Do you think that if Luther and Calvin were alive today, they would find it necessary to begin new religious movements? Why or why not?
3. How has Protestantism influenced America's attitudes toward democracy and free enterprise?

4. How do Roman Catholics and Protestants differ in their fundamental beliefs and practices?
5. How did the closing of monasteries influence the status of Protestant women?
6. Why is devotion to Mary, the mother of Jesus, somewhat controversial?
7. How has the Renaissance and the Enlightenment influenced your education?

WORKS CITED

Luther, Martin. "Lectures on Genesis," in Jaroslav Pelikan, ed., *Luther's Works*, Vol. 1. St Louis: Concordia Press, 1958.

McGrath, Alister. *An Introduction to Christianity*. Oxford: Blackwell, 1997.

Chapter Seven

Christianity in America

$\mathfrak{T}$he New World attracted a wide variety of Christian traditions. Catholic missionaries accompanied the Spanish and French explorers and settlers to care for their spiritual needs. The English settlements made room for Anglicans, Lutherans, Reformed, and a variety of radical Reformation groups. Some of the English settlers left England and Europe seeking religious freedom. None of the religious groups were very successful at permanently converting the Native Americans to their version of the Christian message.

ROMAN CATHOLIC MISSIONARIES

Spain

The beginnings of Christianity in America are often associated with the English colonies and the celebration of the feast of Thanksgiving. Actually the first experience of the indigenous people (misnamed Indians by Christopher Columbus) with Europeans was with Spanish Catholics in the early sixteenth century. The French Catholic missionaries came later in the sixteenth and the English Protestant settlers in the seventeenth century.

Ponce de Leon made the first settlement in St. Augustine, Florida, in 1513, and the Spanish colonists spread along the coast. After a series of problems converting the native population, the Spanish living in the colonies began to intermarry with the Indians and convert them to Roman Catholicism. Attracted by what they thought were great riches, some Spanish explorers ventured to Mexico and the southwestern United States. The explorers were disappointed with the amount of gold they could take out of the Southwest, but the four hundred settlers made friends with the Pueblo Indians, many of whom were baptized. The Franciscan friar, Father Juniper Serra, traveled up the coast of present-day California from Mexico, establishing many missions that still attract pilgrims and tourists today.

Spanish missionaries met with most success in Mexico where a cathedral and a university were built before 1600. Popular devotion to Mary under the title of Our Lady of Guadalupe grew after a native, Juan Diego, had a vision of her and she left an imprint of herself on his cloak. This picture of Mary hangs in the cathedral in Mexico City, where it attracts pilgrims from all the Americas. Gloria Anzaldua (1989), a member of the Mexican Indian community, comments on the significance of Mary as an object of devotion to Americans, Chicanos and Mexicans: "She, like my race, is a synthesis of the old world and the new, of the religion and culture of the two races in our psyche, the conquerors and the conquered" (p. 79). Many shrines to Our Lady of Guadalupe are dotted throughout the Southwest and Mexico and serve as a memorial to the Spanish missionaries.

France

After the creation of Quebec in 1608, French missionaries came to accompany the settlers and the fur traders. The French were less successful than the Spanish at converting the natives, partly because the northern indigenous peoples were so separated geographically from each other, rather than inhabiting towns like the southern Indians.

After the exploration of Father Jacques Marquette and his companion Louis Joliet, French settlements extended from the St. Lawrence River valley, down the Mississippi to New Orleans. Franciscan priests joined the expedition to the Great Lakes region in 1679. Father Louis Hennepin, a Franciscan friar, provided the first written description of Niagara Falls. The Jesuits, or Black Robes as they were popularly called, worked among the native people in central and northern New York State and Ontario, Canada. Some of them were killed by the natives and are venerated today as the North American martyrs. Saints Isaac Jogues, John Brebeuf, Jean de Lalande, Rene Goupil, and Blessed Kateri Tekawitha are remembered today for the dedication and commitment to their faith.

The New Orleans area grew to such proportions that the Ursuline Sisters were sent from France to establish schools for women. More sisters came to staff hospitals and clinics in the area. The French sisters opened similar schools and hospitals in Quebec and Montreal to care for the growing population of the French settlers.

PROTESTANTISM IN THE COLONIES

England

Since most of the first American settlers traced their heritage to England, their religious affiliation was predominately Protestant. The other European Scotch, German, Dutch, and Swedes who arrived later were also members of various Protestant churches, such as Presbyterian, Lutheran, Dutch Reformed, and Calvinist traditions. Many came to escape religious persecution in their homelands; others saw America as the promised land given to the new Israel as part of the covenant with God's people. Just as God had given land and protection to the Israelites, the Jewish chosen people of the Old Testament, God's chosen people of the New Covenant could expect the same consideration.

Anglicans

As head of the Anglican church, the king of England, James I, gave a royal charter to the settlers at Jamestown, Virginia, in 1607. The charter presupposed allegiance to the Church of England, which regulated the worship, doctrine, and discipline as directed by the *Book of Common Prayer.* It was difficult to enforce many of these religious regulations because of the vastness of the territory and the shortage of clergy. The bishop, who lived in England, found it almost impossible to maintain a geographical parish system where he could control the instruction and worship through his appointed minister. The great distance hindered communication with English hierarchy, so more authority was given to the laity. Churches were so distant from each other that sacraments, instruction, and worship were often performed in the homes. As the laity became more involved in the congregations, a system of vestries arose. The vestry consisted of the men of the parish who coordinated the affairs, including the hiring of ministers. The vestries became more powerful as many of them exercised their version of the priesthood of the faithful, controlling finances, buildings, worship, instruction, and the lives of the clergy. Lay involvement in the life of the church became a leading characteristic of American Protestantism that continues today.

Puritans

The Puritans arose as a movement in England in the sixteenth century in opposition to the English church's refusal to purify itself of Roman Catholic elements. They eventually divided into Presbyterians and Congregationalists who still bore the imprint of their parent church. The Puritans suffered persecution from the Anglican Church, and some fled to America on the *Mayflower* in 1620. They considered themselves pilgrims in the biblical sense of people journeying to their heavenly reward. The Puritans based their concept of religion and government on a covenant with God.

Individuals upheld their side of the covenant by correct worship and living upright lives. The congregation upheld its responsibility to the covenant by electing only its own members to government office. Government enforcement of religious activities caused some members to object to the suppression of dissents and violation of conscience. The objectors were perceived as disloyal to the covenant and were excommunicated or banished. One of the objectors, Roger Williams, founded a new colony in Rhode Island, where he welcomed other dissenters, such as Quakers, Baptists, and Anglicans.

RELIGIOUS TOLERATION

Calling the church a "company of worshippers," Roger Williams emphasized its voluntary aspect in contrast to the forced membership of a state religion. William Penn invited wealthy Quakers from England to purchase land in the area presently known as Pennsylvania. Baptist, Scotch-Irish Presbyterians, German Lutherans, and Roman Catholics soon settled in the region. Although Maryland was first seen as a haven for Catholics because it was purchased by the Catholic Lord Baltimore, they were soon outnumbered by Protestants. Eventually it became a place where the two groups could worship unhindered. The Dutch Reformed Church members in New York became more tolerant of diverse religious groups and invited Jewish immigrants who were suffering persecution in Brazil. New York, because of its religious tolerance, attracted settlers of diverse religious traditions such as the Congregationalists, Catholics, Quakers, Mennonites, Baptists, and Lutherans. None of theses religions were sponsored by the state but existed side by side in religious equality. A new concept of church membership developed called "volunteerism," wherein one joined a religious tradition voluntarily and agreed to support it financially. As the colonies expanded, the ideal of religious liberty became a hallmark of the new nation, because individual freedom was grounded in democratic ideals. Religious liberty led to the creation of denominations that respected beliefs and activities of other groups without trying to convert them.

Great Awakening

One of the factors contributing to religious tolerance in America was an eighteenth-century phenomenon called the Great Awakening. Itinerant preachers began the movement in response to what they perceived as spiritual laxity in the Protestant denominations. They traveled the countryside, preaching the need to awaken in the people an awareness of their sin and a need for forgiveness. People from all denominations crossed state lines to attend the religious revival meetings. Many of the meetings were held outdoors, where charismatic preachers inspired their audience to repentance. The preachers appealed to the emotions of their hearers, who often would sway, scream, and pass out spontaneously.

The itinerant preachers met with success in their goal of converting lax Americans to Christ. An unplanned side effect of the Great Awakening was the creation of a national consciousness of Americans as Christians. Most of the colonies still saw themselves as tied to England, and here was an exciting force that bound them together as Americans. The enthusiastic ministers usually preached in the open air rather than confining themselves to churches of a particular denomination. Members of the various religious traditions began to see themselves as all part of God's New Covenant with America as the promised land.

Denominations

Religious tolerance grew in the colonies as Anglicans, Catholics, Baptists, Methodists, Presbyterians, Lutherans, Quakers, and Jews began to live and work side by side. Some of the early American leaders became Deists who believed that a deity had created the world but left humans to care for and develop it. The Deity required the practice of virtue and the avoidance of evil, the consequences of which would be rewarded or punished in the future. George Washington, Thomas Jefferson, and Ben Franklin considered themselves Deists and taught that religion formed moral individuals who would make good citizens. With such a variety of religious traditions in the country, the founding fathers thought it necessary to insure the voluntary practice of religion. They drafted the First Amendment to the Constitution which reads: "Congress shall make no laws respecting the establishment of religion, or prohibiting the free exercise thereof." Since there could be no established state religion as in Europe and Asia, a new form of religious organization developed called the "denomination."

Denominations imply that all religious groups in the United States are equal under law and must be supported financially in a voluntary manner by their members. Denominations required educated ministers who would preach to congregation members who voluntarily chose to attend services. America's first colleges were founded to educate ministers in the various Protestant denominations. William and Mary, Harvard, Yale, Princeton, Dartmouth, Columbia, and Brown all began as seminaries for the formation of ministers from their constituent denominations. They later expanded to become colleges and universities that include lay students.

America's view of the separation of church and state has moved them far from the concept of a state-supported religion. Even though Americans continued to view themselves as Christian and predominately Protestant, they had created a new religious phenomenon that still has penetrated only parts of Western Europe, Western Canada, and Australia.

American denominations were influenced by a European movement called Pietism, which sought to improve one's spiritual development and personal holiness by emphasis on the Bible. They met in groups to pray and discuss the meaning of scripture, which they then tried to apply to their lives. The personal response to this call for holiness was termed a "born again" experience, because the Pietists began anew on their personal journey to God. In America, some Christians seeking more personal holiness through the revelation of sacred scripture and the born-again conversion experience formed new Holiness churches. Other groups specialized in speaking in tongues as a mark of personal holiness. They believe in the gifts of the Spirit as found in the New Testament, including glossolalia (tongues), healing, prophecy, and the discerning of spirits. Others have found their response to the scriptures in the simple living of the early church as interpreted by the Quakers, Mennonites, and Amish.

African-American Churches

Some African Americans wonder if Christianity has liberated or oppressed them as a people. The early colonists were ambiguous toward teaching their slaves about Christianity. Although there were no citations in the Bible actually decrying slavery, there were many references upholding the dignity of the human being made in the image of God. How would the white slave owner apply the teachings of equality before God and Paul's words, "In Christ there are no Jews nor Greeks, male nor female, slave nor free—but all are one in Christ Jesus" (Gal. 3:28)? Slaves were not usually invited into the white churches and had to meet by themselves to express their own religious sentiments. These sentiments were often reflected in their spirituals, which depicted heaven as more than a transcendent reality. Heaven, or sometimes Canaan, represented freedom from their present condition of slavery. Frederick Douglass (1962) pointed out the double meaning of heaven in some of the Negro spirituals: "A keen observer might have detected in our repeated singing of 'O Canaan, sweet Canaan, I am bound for the land of Canaan,' something more than reaching heaven. We meant to reach the North and the North was our Canaan" (p. 159). They often sang spirituals based on the liberation of the Jews by God from slavery in Egypt. When they sang from the Old Testament, "Let my people go," the double meaning applied to their own condition of slavery. When they became free, most of the slaves embraced a form of Protestantism similar to that of their former masters.

Free Black people living in the North had formed their own congregations that were mostly connected to the Baptist and Methodist denominations. After the Civil War, the African Methodist Episcopal Church (AME) and the African Methodist Episcopal Zion church (AME–Zion) sent missionaries from the North to the South to convert the freed slaves. Independent churches were formed that emphasized the African-American religious expression of singing, clapping, chanting, and congregational participation. Black Christians exercised their own leadership of these congregations, learned responsibility for each other, and organized societies to help the poor. Many of the urban African Americans joined Holiness and Pentecostal churches, because they were attracted to the music and style of preaching. The preacher became the leader of the congregation and served as spiritual guide, organizer, and exhorter, partly because the white community accepted him as the voice of the African-American community. For example, Martin Luther King Jr.'s preaching instilled the hope for equality and recognition of Black people that gave impetus to the Civil Rights movement in the 1960s.

It is not surprising that the Civil Rights movement began in the Black churches rather than at the social or government level because the church was the most common place that Black people could call their own. African Americans had the freedom in their own religious institutions to develop leadership, express themselves, and keep alive the hope of full liberation from the segregation imposed upon them by white society. They sang gospel music that often reflected their goals, while their chanting and responses to the preaching and witnessing signified their agreement with the message.

The vast migration of Blacks to urban areas led to changing styles of worship. Some joined Catholic churches or white mainline Protestant denominations in which the form of worship is more formal and less emotional. Even the more staid Catholic and Protestant churches have been affected by the enthusiasm of African-American members who have transformed their worship services with gospel music, clapping, and congregational response. As the clergy and congregations became more educated and moved into American middle-class values, some of the Black churches began to resemble more closely their white counterparts. Some African Americans preferred the intimacy, emotionalism, and style of informal worship of the Pentecostal and Holiness churches, which opened storefront churches in the cities. Presently, myriad denominations of Black churches offer various opportunities for worship to accommodate the pluralistic elements of the African-American population.

Christian Abolitionist and Civil Rights Movements

Statements against slavery based on religious grounds began to emerge in the North by 1830. Theodore Dwight Weld taught his fellow students at Oberlin College to preach against slavery, using the rhetoric of the revivals of the Great Awakening. The Grimké Sisters, Angelina and Sarah, left their Presbyterian church for the Quakers because they were so impressed with the Quaker interpretation of Jesus' teaching to treat others as you wished to be treated. They found this teaching of the golden rule so inconsistent with slavery that they confronted slave owners from their native South Carolina, asking them if they were willing to become slaves. Angelina based her argument against slavery on the moral obligation for everyone to reach moral and spiritual perfection. Since slave owners prohibited their slaves from reaching this goal, they were failing in their moral responsibility. She said that only Christ could be called lord and master, so the slave owners were violating their own religious commitment.

Angelina and Sarah preached, lectured, and wrote that God was the God of the poor and needy, the despised and oppressed. They connected the biblical phrases that supported human rights to women's rights. Both sisters joined the abolitionist movement for the emancipation of slaves but demanded that its policies follow the nonviolent principles of the gospel. The Grimkes recognized the relationship between sexism and racism. They petitioned all women to oppose slavery because they considered slave women as their sisters, whose freedom should be their Christian concern.

The Civil Rights movement was also rooted in Christian churches. The Jim Crow laws that segregated Blacks to the back of the bus, restricted certain areas of restaurants, and separated drinking fountains and restrooms were blatantly discriminatory. Public schools in the 1950s, especially in the South, were segregated. As a result, Black students received a radically inferior education. Although the U.S. Supreme Court had mandated desegregation in public schools, its implementation was very slow in coming. Dr. Martin Luther King Jr., a Baptist minister in Montgomery, Alabama, spearheaded the movement for civil rights for all Americans. His contemporary supporter, Wyatt Walker (1984), comments on King's effectiveness.

> This prince of the church fired our imagination with his novel techniques of nonviolent resistance. The level of our hopes and aspirations were elevated with his splendid oratory and the charisma of his leadership. Within a few years, King had mobilized a non-violent army marching across the South, knocking on the locked doors of justice and equality, demanding with dignity our full citizenship as American-born citizens. (p. 81)

King based his nonviolent approach to civil rights on the teachings and lives of Jesus and Mohandas Gandhi. He and his followers endured ridicule, harassment, and even jail for their efforts to achieve justice and equality. King founded the Southern Christian Leadership Conference in 1957 to organize peaceful protests and demonstrations in favor of civil rights. By 1964, Congress passed the Civil Rights Act with support from Protestant, Catholic, Jewish, and African-American denominations.

Black women often feel marginalized in their churches because although they are recognized for their service, pastors and leaders are usually male. Women's positions are for the most part connected to the traditional feminine roles of Sunday school teachers, nurses, counselors, and deaconesses. Some Black women, along with their white sisters, are still looking for the liberation that their brothers have attained. Although churches teach that equality before God is a basic Christian belief, many women find the ideal beyond their reach.

SUMMARY

America has been considered a Christian country since its first European settlers eyed it as the promised land of the New Covenant. Catholic missionaries from Spain and France attempted to convert the Native Americans and care for the spiritual needs of the explorers they accompanied to the New World. The early English and European settlers usually were members of Protestant denominations and at first established territories for the exclusive use of their own religious traditions. Soon the large immigrant population demanded more religious toleration, which led to the creation of denominations and religious liberty.

The Great Awakening led to the spirit of religious pluralism in America because the camp and outdoor revival meetings avoided denominational churches. The preachers reinforced the belief that all religious traditions were part of God's New Covenant with America. The First Amendment to the Constitution respected the voluntary practice of religion and the equality of all religions before the law. Pietism, a movement which originated in Europe, emphasized the emotional involvement of its members and stressed prayer and study of scripture. Remnants of Pietism can be seen in the Pentecostal and Holiness churches of today.

The African-American churches that had their foundation in slavery retain the spirituals that supported them when they were enslaved. In recent years African Americans have formed their own churches or joined white denominations. Some of the urban Black people have been attracted to Pentecostal and Holiness churches. Black churches became training grounds for Black leadership, producing such men as Martin Luther King and others who helped raise the consciousness of white America to the injustices of segregation.

It was likely that abolitionist and Civil Rights movements should arise in the Christian churches because of the gospel teachings on equality and dignity of humans. Both women and men became active in these movements, which originated in their religious consciousness and were supported by their churches.

DISCUSSION QUESTIONS

1. Why did Christians perceive America as the "Promised Land?"
2. Why was missionary appeal to the Native Americans in the North largely unsuccessful?
3. How did the vestry policy of English colonial churches influence involvement of the laity in Protestant churches?
4. How did the Puritans hinder religious liberty? What beneficial effect did this have in the long run for separation of church and state?
5. How did the Great Awakening contribute to religious tolerance in America?
6. What is the relation of the First Amendment of the Constitution to the following?
   (a) Prayer in public schools
   (b) Tuition wavers for private and parochial schools
   (c) Erection of Christmas displays on public property
7. How are African-American churches related to the experience of slavery?
8. Why did the abolitionist and Civil Rights movements originate in Christian churches?

WORKS CITED

Anzaldua, Gloria. "Entering into the Serpent," in *Weaving the Visions*. Judith Plaskow and Carol Christ, eds., New York: Harper and Row, 1989.

Douglass, Frederick. *Life and Times of Frederick Douglass*. New York: Collier. (Reprinted 1962 [1892]).

Walker, Wyatt Tee. *Soul of Black Worship*. New York: Martin Luther King Fellows Press, 1984.

Chapter Eight

Mainline and Fundamentalist Churches

During the 1920s, American Protestantism experienced dissension between the two groups identified as Modernists, or liberals, and Fundamentalists, or traditionalists. Modernists were called liberal because they tried to adapt church and biblical teachings to the changing intellectual climate. Biblical scholars, working with archaeologists and linguists, found that some of the religious truths based on the Bible did not correlate with new scientific findings. Charles Darwin's (1809–82) *On the Origin of Species* and *Descent of Man,* which provided scientific evidence for the theory of natural selection, gave very little credit to the power of God. Biblical scholars began to apply to the Bible the same critical standards that other forms of literature demanded, researching the biblical authors, their audiences, and their motivation. The critics of these researchers accused the Modernist advocates of this "higher" criticism of ignoring the inspiration of the authors by God. The Modernists found an audience among Catholics and mainline Protestants who found the new scientific approaches to the study of the Bible both interesting and invigorating.

Not all Christians were enthusiastic about the liberal or Modernist approach to the study of the Bible because they thought it violated the fundamental truths of Protestant Christianity. If one could challenge Biblical truths, was one not challenging the very word of God? The opponents to liberal Modernists crossed denominational lines, issuing a series of pamphlets called *The Fundamentals,* in which they outlined their basic beliefs. Most Fundamentalists today adhere to five points: (1) the inerrancy of scripture; (2) the virgin birth of Jesus; (3) the atonement theory of salvation, which is limited to their followers; (4) the bodily resurrection of Jesus; and (5) the literal second coming of Jesus. William Martin (1996) elaborates more fully on the meaning of Fundamentals' doctrines:

> The keystone was and is the inerrancy of Scripture, meaning not only that the Bible is the sole and infallible rule of faith and practice, but also that it is scientifically and historically accurate. Thus, evolution could not be true, miracles really did happen just as the Bible describes them, and on Judgement Day, all who have

ever lived will be assigned for eternity to heaven or hell, both of which really exist. (p. 11)

Fundamentalists emphasize an individual conversion experience, sometimes referred to as being "born again." They define family roles with the father as the breadwinner and the mother at home to care for the children. Fearing the incursion of secularism and pluralism, they advocate private Christian schools and home schooling. They hope that the union of the three socializing institutions of church, family, and school will insure the traditional values so dear to conservative Fundamentalists.

DIFFERENCES BASED ON INTERPRETATION OF SCRIPTURE

Fundamentalists fear that liberals will destroy the authority of the Bible. Protestantism relies on scripture to establish the norms for doctrine and behavior. If followers question the historical accuracy of the Bible, what would happen to the foundations of Protestantism? If one questions the word of God, what will be left of Christianity?

Liberals who employ the historical-critical method of interpretation say that Moses could not have written the first five books of the Old Testament. They point to discrepancies, such as contradictory and duplicate passages written by authors of different traditions. For instance, they note two different creation stories and also question how Moses could write about his own death. Liberals located some geographical inaccuracies in the New Testament and also found some letters ascribed to Paul that were written after his death. They noticed that some historical events in the New Testament did not correlate with extra-biblical literature written at the same time, such as the reigning officials at the time of Jesus' birth.

In reaction to the liberals, some Fundamentalists claimed that because scripture is the word of God and God is infallible, there can be no error in the writings. Some literalists claimed that inerrancy applied to geographical places, historical events, and persons named in the Bible. Because they held that the Bible means every word it says, scripture must be taken literally. It must not only be believed exactly as it is written but must also be applied to life in the same literal manner. For example, if Paul wrote to Timothy (1 Tim. 2:9), "Women are to wear suitable clothes, and to be dressed modestly without braided hair, or gold or jewelry," then some Fundamentalist churches forbade women to wear pants, fancy hairdos, or jewelry to church services. Not all Fundamentalist churches take such directions literally, but they do see biblical injunctions as the norm for behavior. The Fundamentalists' belief in the substitution atonement of Jesus' death has caused many of them to be concerned with salvation. They believe that Jesus died to make up for, or atone for, the sins of humankind, but one cannot receive the grace of atonement unless one accepts Christ. Only those who accept Christ as their personal savior will be assured of heaven and receive the grace to overcome sin. How does one know this is true? From the Bible, so it is most important to believe that it is the inerrant and inspired word of God.

Another religious group, called Evangelicals, interpret the Bible in a fundamentalist or literal manner, yet they distinguish themselves from Fundamentalists. Evangelicals accept some forms of biblical scholarship but apply the teachings to their lives in a literal manner. Religious experience is more important than the proclamation of various doctrines. They emphasize personal prayer and Bible reading, human sinfulness, and the need for rebirth. Evangelicals usually place great importance on witnessing to their conversion experience. Mainline denominational churches such as Catholic, Episcopal, Presbyterian, Lutheran, and some Methodist and Reformed churches usually consider their relationship to God as personal and not to be shared in the witnessing experience. Some Evangelicals have used TV to preach their message of salvation, which usually consists of testifying to one's faith. Evangelicals attempt to convert others to their form of religion, which contrasts with the mainline denominations, whose conversions usually occur through marriage. Evangelicals feel the pressing need to evangelize or preach, because they believe that salvation can only occur through faith in Jesus and the born-again experience.

An example of this differing approach to interpreting scripture can be seen in two concepts of heaven and hell given by Pope John Paul II and Baptist professor, R. Albert Mohler, Jr. The Pope said at a Vatican audience that hell is a state of mind, a self-willed exile from God. Heaven, he said, "is neither an abstraction nor a physical place in the clouds, but a loving and personal relationship with the Holy Trinity." Catholic teaching does not deny that hell may be a geographical spot where God will banish sinners but considers that concept merely a visual aid based on scant biblical concepts. The Pope described what Catholics consider the essence of hell: knowledge that one failed to choose salvation in God. R. Albert Mohler, Jr., president of the Southern Baptist Theological Seminary in Louisville, Kentucky, disagrees with the Pope because he believes that the Bible describes hell as a burning pit. He said, "Jesus spoke of hell as a burning lake, where the worms would not die and the fires would not be quenched. It is all very graphic." Liberals using the historical-critical method of interpreting the Bible from Mark 9:48 say that Gehenna, the word Jesus used for hell, literally *is* a place where the worms never die and the fires are never put out—and refers to the garbage dump located outside Jerusalem.

EFFECTS OF BIBLICAL INTERPRETATION ON SOCIAL AND POLITICAL ISSUES

Creationism Theory

The issue of creationism is also connected to the issue of biblical interpretation. If God did not dictate the first five books of the Bible to Moses, then how did creation as told in Genesis come about? Christianity, as in all religions, looks for answers to the question of where we come from. Discussion of origins is common to all religious groups. If one credits cosmic and human origins to a deity, all of creation takes on a sacred character. If an account of the deity's creative efforts are recorded in sacred scripture, followers hold a special loyalty to the words describing the event.

Darwin's theory of evolution presented a challenge to biblical literature because it posited the development of all life from a single cell which occurred over millions of years ago. Since he did not know about genes, he could not account for the survival of mutations over generations. Neither could he identify the missing link in fossil records between primates and humans. But Darwin's theory of natural selection did provide a credible explanation for the similarities and differences among species. Because the process took millions of years, it contradicted the biblical account of creation by God of the universe, plants, animals, and humans in six days.

Although the theory of evolution established a conflict between science and religion, many Modernists thought the differences could be reconciled. Some thought that God could use evolution as a means of creation. In fact, the biblical account says that plants and animals were created before humans. However, other elements do not correspond with evolutionary theory. Some states in the southern United States prohibited the teaching of evolution in public schools. John Scopes was accused of teaching evolution in his biology class in Tennessee in 1925. In a famous trial, he was accused of breaking the state law by teaching "the theory that denies the story of divine creation of man as taught in the Bible." The legislature of the State of Kansas voted in 1999 that evolution could not be taught in their public schools. Some school textbook publishers have produced two versions of their science books, distributing only the creationist view to the Bible Belt states. Many Christian schools teach only the creationism theory of the universe's beginnings because it is more consistent with the Bible.

Equal Rights Amendment

The Amendment for Equal Rights for women failed to gain support in the areas of the United States dominated by Fundamentalism. Fundamentalists cite as the norm for women certain passages from the Bible that uphold the submission of women to their husbands and direct them to remain at home to care for their children. The letter to the Ephesians, which has been attributed to Paul (although some biblical scholars doubt that he wrote it) says, "Wives should be subject to their husbands as to the Lord, since, as Christ is head of the church and saves the whole body, so is a husband head of his wife, and as the church is subject to Christ, so should wives be subject to their husbands" (Eph. 5: 22–23).

Although this passage seems to demean women, it does give a glimpse of a way of life less confusing than the present, because in it everyone knows his and her roles in society. Some Americans hold a nostalgic longing for the romanticized period of the 1950s where there was less crime, more church attendance, simpler lives, respectful children, and an economic upsurge. Women stayed in the home rather than in the workplace, which represented the traditional or family values of the time. The mother was the homemaker who provided solace, comfort, and encouragement for her family. She taught her children to pray, respect authority, and accompany their parents to church. In this idealized environment, doors remained open and cars left unlocked in the driveway, because everyone agreed on what was morally right and wrong.

A change has occurred since the 1950s in which it seems to some that Americans no longer enjoy the blessings of God because they have endorsed a sinful state of sexual promiscuity, drugs, alcohol, violence, and crime. Many Fundamentalists wonder if God has forsaken His sinful people. Fundamentalists would suggest that Americans might suffer His painful wrath if they do not return to the traditional values of the middle of the century, when women were the heart of the home.

In the Fundamentalist view, women who demand gender equality as promoted by the Equal Rights Amendment are violating not only traditional values but also biblical injunctions. Fundamentalists believed that fathers should be the sole source of financial support for the family, so mothers should not usurp that position. Some Evangelicals and Fundamentalists fear the public school system because it relativizes the role of women. Public schools teach both genders to explore all career possibilities and to develop their potential for meaningful and fulfilling lives.

Fundamentalists fear that public schools erode traditional values because they have abolished prayer and Bible reading in the classroom. The academic study of religion is unacceptable because it presents a neutral position regarding the truths of various religions. When one believes that Christianity is the only true religion, one cannot consider the validity of other religions. Sex education in the public schools presents another challenge because Fundamentalists restrict the use of sex to those who are married. They resent sex education teachers who do not stress the morality of the acts, but allow students to examine their own values regarding their behavior. They oppose abortion and consider women's choice in this issue to be an aberration of biblical teaching. Pornography and sexually suggestive advertising is deplored as a violation of traditional family values.

Homosexuality

Homosexuality violates the belief of most Evangelicals and Fundamentalists that a traditional family consists of father, mother, and children. Sex is performed outside of marriage, which they view as morally wrong. They cite biblical references such as Genesis 19, where the sinful men from Sodom wanted to sexually abuse Lot's two male friends. They were struck blind when they tried to force open the door of Lot's home and had to go away unsatisfied. The town of Sodom was held in derision by the writers of the New Testament with reference to its punishment by God with hail and brimstone raining down on them. Leviticus 18:22 says, "You shall not lie with a man as with a woman; it is an abomination." Paul admonishes Christians in 1 Corinthians 6:9, "People who are immoral or who worship idols or are adulterers or homosexual perverts, or who steal or are drunkards or slanderers, or thieves—none of these will possess the kingdom of heaven."

Liberals point out that homosexual relations are included by Paul in a long list of moral violations, all of which can be forgiven by God. Roman Catholics make the distinction between homosexual orientation, which for some is unchangeable, and homosexual behavior. Some Protestant mainline denominations have commitment ceremonies for homosexuals to live in partnership. Many mainline denominations minister to homosexuals with retreats, hospitality to AIDS patients, church services, and social functions, but most Evangelicals and Fundamentalist do not. Even with the outreach ministry, many homosexuals feel alienated from their churches, which they perceive as unfaithful to the inclusiveness that Jesus taught in the gospel.

The Political Right

Evangelicals and Fundamentalists have extended their religious beliefs to American politics in recent years. TV evangelist Pat Robertson created the Christian Coalition in 1988 as a political lobbying group to elect conservative candidates to public office. Ralph Reed and Randy Tate, who succeeded him, helped the coalition to become the voice of the New Christian Right. Membership in the New Christian Right cuts across denominational boundaries, attracting persons with a conservative stance toward abortion, feminism, homosexuality, and traditional family values. They usually endorse prayer in public schools, home schooling, and a strong military defense system for the country.

The New Christian Right appeals most to white, less-educated, working, and middle-class conservative Christians. An example of their sentiments can be found at a recent Southern Baptist convention. One of the largest denominations in America, the Southern Baptists, passed a resolution condemning Disney Media for promoting alleged pro-homosexual societal values in movies and TV shows. They also advocate the posting of the Ten Commandments in public buildings, which has been implemented in some Southern states.

The Promise Keepers

The Promise Keepers are a typical example of the New Christian Right. Founded in 1990 by Bill McCartney, a former football coach at the University of Colorado, Promise Keepers is an organization of men who meet in large stadiums to hear talks about their roles as husbands and fathers. After an emotional stadium rally, Promise Keepers meet in small groups for further discussion and mutual support of their goals. They make promises committing themselves to honor God and Jesus and to build strong marriages and families through love, protection, and biblical values. They promise to influence the world by converting other men to their mission. Part of their commitment to sexual purity is to condemn abortion. Bill McCartney is known to have spoken at rallies held by Operation Rescue. Trying to impress men with the necessity of reclaiming their role as head of the family, Ed Cole, a speaker at a Promise Keepers rally, said:

> Today's males are pathetic men who have become so weak, so insensitive, so uncommunicative, so irresponsible, that women— the weaker vessel—have had to assume man's God's-given role as leader of the family. If your wife no longer trusts you, she can no longer respect you, or submit to you. (quoted in Spalding, *Christian Century*, 1996, p. 262)

Promise Keepers have received mixed support from institutional churches. Some admire their dedication to male spiritual renewal and provision for a stable family life. Others look with less favor on their anti-feminist policies, patriarchal family structure, lack of dogma other than the promises, and the emotionalism of the large rallies.

SUMMARY

A division occurred within Protestantism, separating Modernists (or liberals) from Fundamentalists (or traditionalists). Much of the division was connected to methods of interpretation of the Bible as defining beliefs and norms for behavior, which is an essential component of Protestantism. Liberals endorsed the historical-critical method of interpretation, while Fundamentalists adhered to the literal method, claiming inerrancy as a policy. Evangelicals and Fundamentalists share some of the same religious views, but the former emphasize witnessing to their born-again experience.

Interpretation of scripture can have many ramifications on social and political issues in America. Creationism versus evolution has caused dissension about the way some states teach science in public schools. It has affected the printing of textbooks and legislation regarding the teaching of evolution. Some states from the U.S. Bible Belt refused to ratify the Equal Rights Amendment on the ground that it violated biblical injunctions regarding the role of women. Nostalgia for the relative stability of the 1950s has caused some Americans to long for the less turbulent times when gender roles were clearly defined. They believe that such clarification was an earmark of traditional family values that the Bible endorsed.

Such traditional family values include sexual abstinence outside of marriage, anti-abortion laws, and belief in the aberration of homosexuality. Sex education in schools is feared because of its neutral stance devoid of moral guidance. Prayer in schools is upheld, as well as home schooling as an alternative to public schools.

Fundamentalists and Evangelicals have influenced politics through the establishment of the New Christian Right, which cuts across denominational boundaries and endorses conservative, traditional values. These values are embodied in groups such as the Promise Keepers, an organization of men who desire to retain and restore the patriarchal elements of traditional families that are reminiscent of an earlier time in American history.

DISCUSSION QUESTIONS

1. Why is there so much consternation over the interpretations of the Bible?

2. Would you call yourself a Fundamentalist or a Modernist in the interpretation of scripture? Give reasons for your answer with some specific examples.
3. Why have different interpretations of scripture so affected American political and social issues? Give some examples.
4. Do you agree with the premises of the Promise Keepers? Are some of them more acceptable than others? Give your reasons.

WORKS CITED

Martin, William. *With God on Our Side: The Rise of the Religious Right in America.* New York: Broadway Books, 1996.

Spalding, John. "Bonding in the Bleachers: A Visit to Promise Keepers." *Christian Century,* March 6, 1996.

Chapter Nine

Christian Spirituality

Which of the following passages do you think most exemplifies a traditional Christian religious experience?

> I would see beside me an angel in bodily form—a type of a vision that I am not in the habit of seeing. . . . He was not tall, but short, very beautiful, his face so aflame that he appeared to be one of the highest angels, who seemed to be all afire. . . . In his hands I saw a long golden spear and at the end of the iron tip, I seemed to see a point of fire. With this he seemed to pierce my heart several times so that it penetrated to my entrails. When he drew it out, I thought he was drawing them with it and he left me completely afire with a great love for God. The pain was so sharp that it made me utter several moans; and so excessive was the sweetness caused by this intense pain that one can never wish to lose it, nor will one's soul be content with anything less than God. It is not bodily pain, but spiritual, though the body has a share in it— indeed a great share. So sweet are the colloquies of love which pass between the soul and God that if anyone thinks that I am lying, I beseech God in His goodness, to give him the same experience.
>
> — Teresa of Avila

> At last by the mercy of God, meditating day and night, I gave heed to the context of the words, "In it, the righteousness of God is revealed, 'He through faith is righteous and he shall live.'" Here I felt that I was altogether born again and entered paradise itself through open gates. There a totally other face of the scriptures showed itself to me. Thereupon I ran through the scriptures from memory. I also found . . . the power of God, with which he makes us strong, the wisdom of God, with which he makes us wise, the strength of God, the salvation of God, and the glory of God.
>
> — Martin Luther

> There was no light in the room; nevertheless it appeared to me as if it were perfectly light. As I went in and shut the door after me, it seemed that I met the Lord Jesus Christ face to face. . . . It

seemed to me that I saw him as I would see any other man. He said
nothing, but looked at me in such a manner as to break me right
down to his feet. I have always regarded this as a most remarkable
state of mind; for it seemed to me a reality, that he stood before me
and I poured out my soul to him. I wept aloud like a child, and
made such confessions that I could with my choked utterance. It
seemed to me that I bathed his feet with my tears; and yet I have
no distinct impression that I touched him that I recollect.

— Charles Finney

All three citations are examples of the variety in Christian religious experience. Teresa was a Carmelite nun who lived in the sixteenth century and wrote about her own spiritual growth in her books,
Way of Perfection and *Interior Castle*. Also in the sixteenth century,
Martin Luther describes in his *Preface to Latin Writings* the impact
on his life of his constant meditation on scripture. Charles Finney, of
the Evangelical tradition and a popular American revival preacher of
the nineteenth century, wrote this account in his *Memoirs*. Although
these writers were members of different religious denominations in
Christianity, they all have some elements in common. They were serious students of the spiritual life, trying to intensify their relationship
with God.

DEVELOPING A RELATIONSHIP WITH GOD

Christian spirituality often refers to one's experience of living
out one's relationship with God. It can also refer to an academic discipline that aids the serious seeker to develop this relationship. The
three writers in the previous examples tried to instruct others in the
spiritual life by writing of their own experiences. Whether it is the
lived experience or attempts to progress in the spiritual life through
academic discipline, Christian spirituality is concerned with the human person in relation to God. This relationship can grow and develop throughout one's whole life. The first part of this chapter is devoted to the experiential dimension of spirituality, the second part to
the academic study that involves methods and techniques.

Spirituality is connected to the action of the Holy Spirit. Paul defined the Holy Spirit as the "Lord and Giver of Life" (2 Cor. 3:6), the
third Divine Person who leads believers to the Triune Godhead. For
Paul, the Holy Spirit is central to Christian belief and life because it is
Christ's own Spirit in whose power he was raised from the dead (Rom.
9:11). This same Spirit now dwells in Christians, giving them joy,
peace, and freedom (Rom. 14:17). The Spirit unites the believers so in-

timately to Jesus that they even have a new power to pray (Rom. 8:26). Augustine said that the Spirit is given to believers as the intimate bond of love uniting them to God and to one another. Christians believe that they can cultivate the life of the Spirit within them, which will help them to intensify their relationship with God.

There are many varieties of Christian spiritualities because of the diversity of Christian experiences. Some emphasize emotional responses to the action of the Spirit, some meditate on the word of God, some involve themselves in causes to promote social action, and some quietly reflect on God's goodness in their lives. A general tendency that can be applied to most spiritual seekers is the attempt to deal with the complexities and mystery of human existence. Christian denominations try to impart to their adherents an understanding of the spiritual life in its inner dimension, at the same time keeping their commitment to communal experience or to social and political action.

CHRISTIAN EXPERIENCES OF SPIRITUALITY

Most recent descriptions of spirituality connect it to healthy personality development because a human's spiritual growth helps one to gain a more fulfilling and abundant life. All religions hold the promise of happiness, peace, and fulfillment. Christians believe that the Holy Spirit can help them to achieve this goal by inspiring them to live in a manner that is consistent with the teachings of Jesus. They think that the teachings and example of Jesus provide Christians with the ideal model for spiritual growth. Jesus lived in close relationship with God, and Christians believe that they can do the same.

Developing any relationship takes time and energy, and Christians think that these elements are relevant to their relationship with God. Since all relationships are based on experience, Christians reflect on it as they begin their spiritual journey. Growth usually implies change in one's behavior that is precipitated by a change in attitude. Just as motivation is required for any action, it is also necessary for spiritual growth. Christians believe they can stimulate the growth of motivation by reflecting on their own experiences of the supernatural. For instance, if one's experience of God in the past is that God has been generous, one can build a relationship with God based on gratitude and trust.

Spiritual growth is connected to the human maturation process. Just as humans mature physically, emotionally, mentally, and socially, Christians believe they also develop spiritually. Humans are more than body and mind—they have a distinct spirit that can stagnate or grow. When an individual's spirit is united to the Spirit of the Divine, Christians believe that this harmonious relationship should overflow into their relations with others. As the relationship with God deepens, the seekers of spirituality notice that they begin to experience more peace and harmony in their human relationships.

Christians find a variety of paths to God, because they do not all experience life in the same way. Some have turned away from material goods and consumerism to focus on spiritual growth in their lives. Others have devoted themselves to causes that alleviate the sufferings of the poor and powerless. The path of prayer and study has sufficed for some, and emphasis on personal salvation and healing has been the choice of others. Still others emphasize the conversion experience while some enjoy the ecstatic experiences, such as speaking in tongues. Some people prefer to ponder the actions of God in small groups. They find there a forum to reflect on their faith, home, and work lives with like-minded individuals who share the same values. Some groups stress reflection and prayer, some are devoted to social action causes, and some wish to change the structures that cause injustice and suffering. These groups offer a sense of belonging for the members that seek spiritual growth in the company of others.

Different denominations provide a variety of religious experiences. Roman Catholic and some mainline Protestant denominations usually help their members to achieve a relationship with God through a gradual participation in the life of the church. The sacramental system of participation through Baptism, Communion, Confirmation, Marriage, and Anointing of the Sick helps Catholics and some Protestants to grow gradually in their faith commitment. Some Protestant denominations stress dramatic conversion experiences in which people change their lives to reorient themselves toward God. Howard Thurman (1963), a theologian of the Reformed persuasion, says that the convert, although feeling unworthy, is able to accept the grace of God: "For many, this is the encounter with the living Christ and in his name or in his Spirit, they go forth into newness of life" (p. 23). Comments from persons undergoing the conversion experience include references to being born again and starting their lives over.

Some church members have undergone the more ecstatic experiences of speaking in tongues, of healings, and of prophecy. They feel that the Spirit has entered their lives and touched them in a positive way. Individuals may also experience the presence of the power or the beauty of God when they watch a sunset or a rainbow. A visit to the Grand Canyon or Niagara Falls can instill such a sense of wonder that some persons can feel drawn out of or can transcend themselves as they ponder the wonders of creation.

Spirituality and the Paschal Mystery of Christ

Suffering seems to be part of human existence, but it does not have to be a meaningless experience. Reflecting on the sufferings of Christ helps the spiritual seeker to cope with the daily problems of personal life as well as the larger issues that afflict all of human-kind. The unique contribution of Christianity to an understanding of suffering and evil is that Christians believe they have a God who suffers with them. However, they believe that the suffering of Jesus, both in his life and in his crucifixion, was not in vain. Because of that suffering and death, Christians believe that Jesus and all his followers can experience new life with God through resurrection. Considering the sufferings of Christ, Christians encounter God not only in joy, peace, truth, and beauty, but also in sorrow, pain, loss, and ignorance. Believers are convinced that by conforming their lives to the life and death of Jesus, they too will receive eternal life. By participating in the paschal mystery, or the death and resurrec-tion of Christ, Christians encounter God. Hans Kung (1977), a noted theologian, said, "The God manifested in Jesus is . . . a God encoun-tering man as redeeming love, identifying Himself in Jesus with suf-fering man" (p. 435).

This loving God has provided Christians with a model for cop-ing with evil in their own lives. Although much suffering is caused by external circumstances, some of it arises from the compulsions, ob-sessions, and desires of the individual. Rather than blaming others or circumstances beyond their control, Christians know that their own passions can be blamed for much of their sufferings. By focusing on the paschal mystery, or the suffering, death, and rising of Christ, they notice a downward and upward movement. He died, was buried and rose again. Christians likewise can die to their inclinations that cause their faults so they can rise to new life with Christ. By examin-ing their own use of their passions, Christians can evaluate whether they are employed for constructive or selfish ends.

Although Jesus died on the cross and was raised to life again only once, Christians believe that he, like themselves, had to undergo daily many small deaths and risings during his life on earth. He had to suffer hunger before the satisfaction of food. He had to undergo the frustration of the ignorance and misunderstandings of his followers, the false accusations of his enemies, and the misinterpretations of his words and deeds. Yet he was able to overcome these evils because of his love for God that overflowed to his love for humans. Basing their lives on the example of Christ, Christians also apply the dying–rising motif of the paschal mystery to their lives. Believers sometimes find that their passions can be both a help and a hindrance to spiritual growth. Without passions, life could be unproductive, dull, and boring, but passions out of control can cause much sorrow to oneself and to others.

The Passions: Helps and Hindrances to the Spiritual Life

Buddhism calls the passions ignorant cravings that must be extinguished before one can grow spiritually. Christians take this action one step further by transforming the negative aspects of their passions into positive concerns for others. In dying to the negative aspects of passions, Christians hope to rise to their more beneficial elements. Some of these passions can be obstacles to spiritual growth if they do not adhere to the Christian message. Pride, greed, anger, lust, gluttony, envy, and sloth have been called capital sins or passions that can be a hindrance to spiritual growth and human maturation.

Some people find that many of their troubles are influenced by a false sense of pride, which causes them to rely on their own efforts and resources to attain happiness. Although initiative is commendable, it can become a source of self-sufficiency that instills ideas of success without the help of God or others. In order to die to selfish pride, Christians try to become more dedicated to self-sacrificing service to others. They believe that only by serving others may they resemble Jesus, who said that he came not to be served but to serve others.

Humans find that they must also die to their tendency to greed. The passion of greed causes much evil in this world because of its relation to materialism, imperialism, and consumerism. Some people soothe hurt feelings and disappointments by going shopping. There is an immediate gratification to accumulating material goods, but it does not satisfy for long periods of time. Christians find that the need to accumulate goods does not substitute for the lack of human relations or relationship with God. In trying to die to greed, the spiritual seeker tries to rise to generosity. Instead of hoarding goods for oneself, the Christian tries to distribute them to the needy. On a personal level, the Christian will work in food pantries, soup kitchens, used clothing "closets," and other facilities that distribute goods to the less fortunate. On a social level, the Christian would send money to organizations that help the poor or work to change the political and social structures that cause the disparity between the rich and poor.

Envy is related to greed in that one perceives that others have more than oneself and so one wishes either that the person who is the object of one's envy would become deprived of the assumed good or that the perceiver would receive the same thing. Envy can destroy harmonious relationships and lead to loneliness and sorrow. In trying to die to envy, the Christian wishes for the good of another. Rising to new life might involve helping the envied ones to attain their goals.

Anger, like all human passions can be used for good. Jesus himself showed anger with the religious authorities in Israel when they censored him for curing a man on the Sabbath (Mk. 3:6). Anger usually results from a hurt or a slight that victims feel have been dealt to them unjustly. This anger can result in physical aggression or verbal abuse directed at the perceived cause of the hurt, or it can be directed toward an innocent victim who cannot understand the outburst. When one dies to anger, one tries to rise to compassion. Jesus showed compassion in many instances, such as his friendship with Zaccheus, the hated tax collector who turned his life around after their encounter. The unknown woman who was a public sinner in Luke 7:36 received his compassion in the home of the condemning Pharisee. Yet, anger can be justified in some situations of injustice, such as harm done to the innocent. Some Christians are motivated to work for social justice issues and peace activities because of their anger at the inequalities and injustices in our societies.

Lust is another passion that unchecked can cause sorrow and pain. It can be used to exploit others for one's own personal gain and satisfaction. But without this gift of procreation, humans would not survive on this earth. Christians believe that sex is a gift of God to be used not to exploit but for the benefit of self and others.

By dying to the misuse of their passions, Christians believe they will be dying to their selfishness. In rising to the unselfish and constructive use of these passions as Jesus did, they will find their true selves, which is the life of God within. Christians believe that they cannot find themselves in isolation from humankind, as Thomas Merton (1961), a noted mystic, said, "For it is precisely in the recovery of our union with our brothers (and sisters) in Christ that we discover God and know Him, for then His life begins to penetrate our souls and His love possess our faculties and we are able to find out who He is from the experience of His mercy, liberating us from the prison of self concern" (p. 78).

AN ACADEMIC STUDY OF
CHRISTIAN SPIRITUAL PRACTICES

Some Christians wish to identify stages in spiritual growth that would correlate with stages of growth in other areas of their lives. Although not all spiritual seekers prefer a designated route, some find the experience of others who are considered masters in the spiritual life to be helpful to their spiritual journey. A paradigm has been developed by spiritual writers that can help some Christians advance in their relationship with God. Some spiritual seekers have found the schema useful while others prefer a more natural approach. The steps are flexible and often overlap. Some experiences, such as spontaneous prayer, penetrate through all the steps and continue through all the journey.

Prayer

Prayer has been defined as the expression of one's relationship with God. Just as humans intensify their relationships with one another by dialogue, Christians believe they can communicate with God through prayer. Sometimes this prayer takes the form of petition, when one asks for help or favors from God. Christian prayer may involve thanksgiving for God's gifts, or it can be an expression of sorrow for failure. Praises for the wonder of God's gifts often are uttered as prayer. Sometimes Christians prefer to pray alone and at other times to share their prayer with a community at public ceremonies. Students of spirituality say that the quality of private prayer often determines the quality of public prayer and can prevent some of the boredom claimed by participants who engage in communal worship.

Usually, spiritual seekers mature in their understanding of prayer in the same way as they mature in other areas of development. Just as the child learns to speak in words by imitating the words of others, Christians begin to pray by saying the words of prayer that were taught to them by others, such as the Lord's Prayer. This form of prayer has the advantage of giving the tools and vocabulary to initiate one's verbal relationship with God. Then, Christians can move to using their own words in a spontaneous expression of wonder, sorrow, gratitude, or petition. The prayer of petition can be controversial because it sometimes indicates that Christians want to get something from God. There is lurking the suggestion that those who pray are trying to change the mind of God. John Calvin (1960) said we pray, "that our hearts may be fired up with a burning desire ever to seek, love and serve God" (p. 897). Rather than trying to change the mind of God, those who pray seek to change themselves by stimulating and strengthening their faith. They try to be open to the will of God, which they perceive is the best for them. Recalling the words of Paul in Romans 8:28, they believe that "all things work to good for those who love God." The next sections will focus on private prayer by explaining meditation, the Jesus prayer, contemplation, and mysticism.

Meditation. Christian meditation is considered a discursive prayer in that the intellectual dimensions of reason or thinking dominate. A typical meditative prayer will take some time as the person focuses on the presence of God, both in the scriptures and in one's life experience. One examines one's own goals, hopes, and objectives and tries to see how consistent they are with the gospel values. Then one tries to reflect on these values in order to discover how to incorporate them into one's life.

A typical form of meditative prayer has been taught by the Jesuits, a religious order known for their intellectual pursuits. It has been passed down by their founder, St. Ignatius of Loyola who lived in the sixteenth century. He taught that one should read the scriptures, reflect on them as they apply to one's personal life, and then decide how one would change one's own life to conform more to the life of Christ. For example, in the gospel of Mark, one would read the story of Jesus being rejected by his own people as he spoke in the synagogue in Nazareth.

> On the Sabbath day he began to teach in the synagogue. Many people went there and when they heard him, they were astonished, saying, "Where did this man get all this? What is the wisdom given to him? What mighty works are wrought by his hands? Is not this the carpenter, the son of Mary, and are not his brothers, James, Judas, Joses and Simon and his sisters here with us?" And they rejected him. Jesus said to them, "A prophet is not without honor, except in his own country, and among his own kin and in his own house." He was not able to perform any miracles there except that he laid his hands on a few people and healed them. He was surprised at their unbelief, but went about other villages continuing to teach.
>
> (Mk. 6:1–6)

Christian believers would notice the rejection and disappointment that Jesus must have felt. They then would consider a time in their own lives when they had been rejected for any reason. They would compare Jesus' reaction with their own reaction to rejection. Then they would decide to act in a manner similar to Jesus, who did not allow rejection to deter him from his teaching about the kingdom of God. They usually would close by asking God for help to keep their resolution to conform their lives to that of Christ. This is an intellectual experience using one's ability to read the scriptures, reflect on them, and act upon them as applied to life. Ignatius taught that frequent meditation on the gospels would increase one's knowledge of Christ and one's desire to model one's life on him.

Meditation is not restricted to reflection on scripture. One can meditate on nature and reflect on God's goodness and providential care for humans. Brilliant sunsets, rainbows, and starlit skies can provoke awe and wonder at the complexity of God. One can meditate on one's own and the universe's origins, trying to plumb the actions of God. Meditation on the human body and its interdependent networks can suggest to Christians that they depend upon a superior intellect who could create such a marvel of efficiency. Finally, as Christians meditate on the universe and its interconnected systems, they might realize their dependence on God and each other as they travel their spiritual journey together.

The Jesus Prayer or Centering Prayer. Some students of the spiritual life find an easy transition from meditation to contemplative prayer by employing the techniques of the Jesus prayer. This form of prayer originated in the Orthodox branch of Christianity and has found popularity recently in the West. It is sometimes called centering prayer because the person attends to the presence of God within, that is, at the center of one's being. When one is practicing centering prayer, one usually employs a mantra or phrase that one repeats over and over again.

The Jesus prayer usually begins with breathing exercises to help one relax and focus. Those practicing the prayer start with an image of Jesus that is important to their experience. Using their imagination, they speak to Jesus about their needs and concerns. Then they listen for the response of Jesus. Instead of a monologue as in meditation, those who pray take prayer a step further and try to establish a dialogue with Jesus. Howard Rice (1991), a theologian of the reformed tradition, says, "We need to pray as both speakers and hearers. We speak to the Other and we listen for the Other to address us" (p. 85). The centering prayer can also be less visual and more oral, using mantras to keep one's attention in focus. The mantra-like prayer usually consists of "Lord Jesus Christ, have mercy on me." The person praying repeats this prayer many times, attending to the presence of God within, that is, at the center of one's being. By going beyond images and listening with the heart, some exponents of the spiritual life feel they can be more in contact with Christ.

Contemplation. Contemplation is also known as affective prayer. Theologian Karl Barth (1952) said, "Prayer must be an act of affection; it is more than a question of using the lips, for God asks the allegiance of our hearts. If the heart is not in it, if it is only a form carried out more or less correctly, what is it then? Nothing!" (p. 26). Contemplative prayer allows those who pray, total persons composed of intellect, imagination, emotions, and body, to respond to God using the whole self, mind, imagination, and affections. It is believed that contemplation is not a method of prayer to be chosen at will, but a gift of God to which one is drawn. Some Christians believe that meditation and the Jesus prayer prepare the individual to hear this call as those who pray become more familiar with the ways of God.

Teresa of Avila, a fifteenth-century mystic, writes of contemplatives engaged in prayer, "They seem not to be in this world, and have no wish to see or hear anything but their God; nothing distresses them nor does it seem that anything can possibly do so. In short, for as long as this state lasts, they are so overwhelmed and absorbed by the joy and delight which they experience that they can think of nothing else to wish for" (1961, p. 202). Thomas Keating (1997), a Trappist monk, says that "as Christians relate to the passion, death and resurrection of Christ, they are not relating to something outside of themselves, but to something inside. They can identify with Christ in his temptations in the desert, his agony in the garden, and his sufferings on the cross" (p. 34). He indicates that the goal of contemplative prayer is not so much the emptiness of thoughts or conversation as it is the emptiness of self. "A different kind of knowledge rooted in love emerges in which the awareness of God's presence supplants the awareness of our own presence and the inveterate tendency to reflect upon ourselves" (p. 35). In contemplative prayer the emphasis for Christians is not on goals, motivations, or actions, but on Christ.

Christians believe this relationship with God that grows from contemplative prayer resembles the relationship of two lovers or very good friends. When one knows that one is loved and affirmed by another, neither person needs always to make use of words. They can just relax and enjoy one another's presence. Teresa of Avila referred to this situation as "wasting time with God." One does not expect to accomplish anything, but just to stay in the presence of the Other. Often contemplatives experience feelings of consolation and affirmation that make them want to prolong the moments of prayer. However, spiritual writers warn that the effects on those who pray are not shown in their enjoyment but rather in their unselfish treatment of others. Teresa claimed that the benevolent treatment of others verified the contemplative experience as those who pray became loving persons in a loving community.

Contemplative prayer often begins with scripture. When meditating on a passage such as the Agony in the Garden, the contemplative would attempt to identify with the person of Jesus and imagine themselves in the garden with him. They would listen and then talk to him and try to experience the feelings, frustration, and disappointment of Jesus knowing that he would be abandoned by his friends, family, and the people he served. With words of comfort, they would try to console Jesus in his agony, sharing their love and affection for him. The emphasis of this prayer would not be on the person contemplating but on Jesus, with whom they identified.

Other types of contemplative prayer might not use words at all, but just enjoyment of the relationship with God that enables the contemplative to relish the shared silence. Just as friends do not always need to talk to reinforce their presence, one does not need to use one's intellect, imagination, or emotions to indulge softly in the presence of the Divine. Teresa of Avila could even tease and play with God. One time when she was riding a horse to visit a bishop, the horse fell and spilled her into the muddy water. She told God that it was no wonder that He had so few friends because of the way He treated them. Contemplative prayer motivates the spiritual seeker to initiate and complete intimacy with God, but the seekers realize that they must wait for God to grace them with this opportunity.

Mysticism. Spiritual writers who follow the schema of spiritual growth progressing from prayer through meditation and contemplation, consider mystical prayer as the culmination or pinnacle of spiritual development. Others feel that God can favor individuals with the mystical experience at any time. Evelyn Underhill (1964), a twentieth-century Christian writer on mysticism, defines mysticism as the "direct intuition or experience of God: and a mystic is one who has had direct experience—one whose religion and life are centered, not merely on accepted belief and practice but on that which one regards as personal firsthand knowledge" (p. 10). One does not receive this knowledge from books or teachers, although this academic form of knowledge can provide a starting point. Mystical knowledge is infused by God as a direct experiential knowledge of the Divine. The experience can be so overwhelming that mystics have decried their lack of vocabulary to describe it. They say that there are no words in the human language that can adequately convey the beauty, truth, and love that was given to them. The mystical experience engenders a strong sense of unity and harmony with God, self, others, and the environment.

The mystic returns from the intimate experience of God energized and socially active. Richard Woods (1981), a spiritual writer, says mysticism "is a supernormal style of life in which the further reaches of human nature are approached and even surpassed" (p. 21). Most mystics do return from their experience with a new vitality and strength to enter the practicalities of everyday living. They do not care to call attention to themselves or their mystical experience, as witnessed in the lives of Dag Hammarskjöld or Tom Dooley, who wrote how their mystical experiences made them more available for others. Many Christian mystics renounce their worldly possessions in order to become one with God's poor and oppressed. Mystics appear to be well adjusted and integrated human beings because they constantly project to others their harmonious unity with God, themselves, others, and their environment.

Discipleship: Prayer and Action

Prayer and action are considered complimentary dimensions of a full Christian life. Christians look to the example of Jesus, a man of prayer, who went off to pray by himself in order to be in prayerful union with his Father. Luke and Matthew show him teaching his disciples to pray and to address God as Father. Prayer and action were intertwined for Jesus. The gospel writers portray him as praying alone and with others, yet leaving that prayer whenever the service of others was required. In his teaching and actions, Jesus stressed the connection between love of God and love of neighbor.

Martin Luther (1483–1546) taught the ideal of spiritual integration of prayer and action of a disciple of Christ. By stressing the universal priesthood of all the baptized, he underscored the need of cultic or shared ritual prayer. But this prayer was to be joined with service to God and to members of the community. He said that in the quest for holiness, even secular pursuits could be enriched by personal and communal prayer.

Ignatius of Loyola (1491–1556) developed a comprehensive and integrated spirituality of prayer and apostolic service. He claimed that authentic faith led to service, and that true love manifests itself in deeds as well as words. He advocated contemplative prayer in action, in which prayer and service to others were linked.

Christians can be energized and motivated through prayer to share their vision with others. They believe that as they grow in the spiritual life, they will be liberated from self-centeredness, so they can direct their energy to the selfless service of others. Martin Luther King Jr. (1964) illustrates the need to blend prayer and action in his plea for strength to continue his work for civil rights:

> It seemed to me that all of my fears had come down on me at once. I had reached the saturation point. . . . In this state of exhaustion, when my courage had almost gone, I determined to take my problem to God. I prayed aloud . . . and experienced the presence of the Divine as I never before had experienced him. . . . Almost at once my fears began to pass from me. My uncertainties disappeared. I was ready to face anything. The outer situation remained the same, but God had given me an inner calm. (p. 229)

Mother Teresa of Calcutta is another example of prayer-seeking action. She claimed that when she looked upon the face of a human being, she could see the image of God. This vision enabled her to bathe, feed, clothe, and shelter many of the unfortunates in India.

Small faith communities have helped some Christians to integrate the union of prayer and action into their lives. Some people find spiritual satisfaction by sharing their faith with one another, often by reading and meditating on scripture. They find that like-minded individuals who share their values and aspirations will work together to establish food pantries, soup kitchens, homeless shelters, and other forms of social action. Some of these small faith communities branch out to the political arena in order to change the structures that cause social and economic injustice. They derive their strength and faith from their group prayer that enables them to work unselfishly for others.

SUMMARY

Christian spirituality is concerned with the person's relationship with God. One can approach the study of spirituality from one's life experience or from the traditional stages of spiritual growth. Reflecting on their life experiences can motivate Christians to examine their life of the Spirit. Diverse life experiences can lead to different religious experiences, such as ecstatic, conversion, or gradual progress through the sacraments, which enable the student to grow in the spiritual life.

One of the great challenges to spiritual growth is the meaning of suffering. Christians realize that much of their suffering is caused by their own thoughtless compulsions that are rooted in their passions. These passions can be utilized for good or evil depending upon the inclinations of the individual. Following the death–resurrection motif of the paschal mystery, Christians can transform those passions into a love of God and service to others. By dying to their selfishness and egocentrism, they can discover their true selves, which is the life of God within.

The traditional academic study of religion suggests that there are stages through which Christians progress as they intensify their relationship with God. They start at the levels of rote and spontaneous prayer and progress through meditation, the Jesus prayer, and contemplation, to mysticism. Meditation employs the intellectual faculties of memory, understanding, and will. The Jesus prayer introduces one to contemplative prayer by stimulating the imagination to help the individual engage in a dialogue with God. Contemplative prayer brings the spiritual seeker closer to God in that one can rest in God's presence and enjoy the intimacy that it brings. Mysticism is traditionally considered the culmination of the spiritual journey because the individual experiences an intuitive knowledge and presence of God, which bestows a sense of union with God, self, others, and the environment. The test of the mystical experience is the caring concern for others that determines the validity of the spiritual life based on the model of Christ.

Most Christian denominations connect prayer to action. Some members find small faith communities within their denominations where they can share their spiritual journey and engage in social action.

DISCUSSION QUESTIONS

1. What is meant by spirituality, and how is it connected to the Holy Spirit?
2. How is spirituality connected to the maturation process?
3. Why is there such diversity in religious experience? Give some examples.
4. Why is the Paschal Mystery of Christ a good model to help individuals on their spiritual journey?
5. How can one say that one's passions can be utilized for good or evil depending on the inclination of the individual?
6. What is the importance of prayer in one's spiritual journey?
7. Why has meditation been called an intellectual effort? What are its benefits?
8. How does the Jesus prayer prepare one for contemplation?
9. Why is mysticism called by some the pinnacle of spiritual development?
10. Illustrate the concept of prayer combined with action, using concrete examples.

WORKS CITED

Avila, Teresa. *Interior Castle,* trans. E. Allison Peer. Garden City, NY: Image Books, 1961.

Barth, Karl. *Prayer According to the Catechism of the Reformation: Stenographic Record of Three Seminars,* adapted A. Roulen, trans. Sara Terrien. Philadelphia: Westminister, 1952.

Calvin, John, in John McNeill (ed.), *Institutes of the Christian Religion,* trans. Ford Lewis Battles. Philadelphia: Westminister, 1960, III, XX, p. 34.

Finney, Charles. *Memoirs.* New York: A. S. Barnes, 1876.

Keating, Thomas. *Intimacy with God.* New York: Crossroads, 1997.

King, Martin Luther, Jr. *Strength to Love,* in *A Martin Luther King Treasury.* Yonkers, NY: Educational Heritage, 1964.

Kung, Hans. *On Being a Christian.* New York: Doubleday, 1977.

Luther, Martin. "Lectures on Genesis" in Jaroslav Pelikan (ed.), *Luther's Works,* Vol. 1. St. Louis: Concordia Press, 1958.

Merton, Thomas. *New Seeds of Contemplation.* New York: New Direction, 1961.

Rice, Howard. *Reformed Spirituality.* Louisville: Westminster, John Knox, 1991.

Thurman, Howard. *Disciplines of the Spirit.* New York: Harper and Row, 1963.
Underhill, Evelyn. *The Mystics of the Church.* New York: Schocken, 1964.
Woods, Richard. *Mysterion.* Chicago: Thomas Moore Press, 1981.

Chapter Ten

Christian Economic
and Social Justice

JUSTICE, EQUALITY, AND HUMAN RIGHTS

Christians in developed countries are becoming more alarmed by the emphasis on individualism, where individual interests take preference over the needs of the community. The initiation ritual of Baptism calls Christians to community, emphasizing a caring and sharing attitude toward others. Individualistic tendencies cause people to be preoccupied with themselves, their comfort, and their economic gain rather than with concern for the good of others. Concentration on the rights of the individual often causes Christians to ignore the social sinful situations produced by governments and other institutions. Such social sins of poverty, racism, sexism, and economic and social deprivation can easily become forgotten by those Christians and others who are concerned with only their personal well-being. Many Christians see the need to apply principles of Christian economic and social justice in order to change the structures that cause these larger evils or social sins.

Christians trace their concern for social and economic justice to the Bible with its many references to human rights. The Bible states that all persons are created in the divine image of God and therefore are equal in worth, dignity, and fundamental rights. Christians believe that all humans have the responsibility to participate in the political, social, and economic decisions that affect their lives. All people are entitled to share in the fruits of the earth, which in turn calls everyone to care for and preserve nature. Christians believe that all of life exists within the sphere of God's care and judgment; individuals, institutions, and governments are subject to moral accountability. Since the earth is God's, its resources must be used for the benefit of all, not just for a privileged minority.

Following the example of Jesus the Redeemer, Christians believe that people living in oppression, poverty, and helplessness should be aided and empowered to regain their human dignity. They quote the gospel of Matthew, chapter 25, which says that nations and peoples will be judged by God on how they treat the hungry, the homeless, and the most vulnerable members of society. Believers are obliged to question institutions, governments, and businesses that oppress others for their own gain and then to strive to change the structures that are the causes of injustices. For example, a bank in Buffalo, New York, redlined an upper-middle-class neighborhood. Redlining means that banks will refuse to lend money to prospective buyers of homes whom they would consider undesirable, such as African Americans, single mothers, or homosexuals. When the Catholic and Protestant parishioners of that neighborhood learned of this practice, they immediately organized and threatened to remove all their money from the bank if it did not change its policy. The bank refused. The money was removed; the bank failed and had to leave the city. Christians acting on principles of social justice were able to influence an institution that was depriving humans of their dignity.

The National Conference of Catholic Bishops published a document on economic justice in 1997. They said that all economic life should be shaped by moral principles. Institutions must be judged on how they protect or undermine the life of the human person, support the family, and serve the common good. This means that all people should have the right to life and to secure the basic human necessities of life, that is, food, clothing, shelter, education, health care, a safe environment, and economic security. The bishops recognized the interconnectedness of all peoples on the planet. They see that globalization of the economy can bring enhanced economic growth in many parts of the world, yet the gap between rich and poor continues to widen. Critical thinkers are questioning capitalism as the only economic model for peoples of the Third World. The U.S. media have exposed poor working conditions, low salaries, unsuitable housing, and oppression of workers by American companies whose primary goal is profit.

One of the concerns of many mainline Catholics and Protestants that might serve as an example of applying Christian principles to a social situation is the cancellation of debt burden on poor countries. Because of the huge debt that poor countries owe to rich countries, the World Bank and the International Monetary Fund are depriving people of fundamental human services. The *Quarterly Bulletin* of Oxfam International (1999) said, "Debt repayments have meant health centers without drugs or trained staff, schools without basic teaching equipment, and the collapse of agricultural extension services. Families in poor villages and urban slums are unable to maintain health and nutritional standards and are unable to keep their children in school" (p. 2). The obligation to meet debt repayments often means that aid from other countries like the United States, which was meant for improving education, health care, and social services, is used to refinance debt payments. Foreign governments are less likely to make investments in companies that would promote economic growth in poor countries because they know all the profits will be used for debt reduction, rather than for helping workers to become consumers.

Since our world is increasingly interconnected, social, economic, and environmental problems in some countries threaten the well-being of people everywhere. The environment is not exempt from maltreatment by attempts to repay the world debt. Farmers deplete the nutrients from their land by overusing it to plant cash crops for export. Mineral and forest reserves are exhausted by questionable mining techniques and extreme cutting without reforestation. Because the impoverished people have less money to buy goods from industrialized nations, their exports diminish, causing loss of jobs at home. The Jubilee year of 2000 was designated by mainline Catholic and Protestant denominations as the year to cancel all debts as they were cancelled every fiftieth year in the Old Testament. Slaves were allowed to go free, land was left unplowed, and even the animals were not forced to work. Considering the Judeo-Christian heritage of mercy and compassion, many mainline Christians are making efforts to influence governments, banks, and businesses to cancel debts owed by poor countries.

Another example of Christian social justice is concern for immigrants. Globalization has raised the consciousness of the plight of displaced persons and refugees. Faith-based organizations associated with the World Council of Churches, the Lutheran World Federation, the Quaker United Nations Office, the International Catholic Migration Office, and Caritas International have tried to improve the plight of the refugee. They have advised the United Nations about the needs of displaced persons, both those within countries' boundaries and those sent to other countries during war. Many groups have solicited funds from their members to relieve the sufferings of the poor by working with other nongovernmental organizations located within the areas affected by war, famine, earthquakes, floods, revolutions and other upheavals.

MOVEMENTS TO HELP WORKERS AND THE POOR

Concern for human dignity became connected to the Christian mandate to spread the kingdom of God. This concern inaugurated a movement called the Social Gospel, in which the kingdom is perceived not only as a spiritual reality but also as a transformation of human society where poverty, homelessness sickness, and ignorance would be overcome. The Social Gospel was two-pronged: one arm was directed to immediate rescue help for the poor and the needy; the other was aimed at transforming society so that the kingdom of God could begin on earth.

The direct aid to the needy began with rescue efforts from Protestant churches to help the underprivileged. Jane Addams's Hull House in Chicago was an example of a place where women provided social services, and classes in sewing and cooking, and attempted to integrate immigrants into American society. Many modern churches show their concern for the poor by housing food pantries, used clothes "closets," dining rooms, and shelters where the needy can benefit from their services. Churches of all denominations provide chaplains to hospitals, prisons, and colleges to attend to the spiritual needs of patients, prisoners, and students. Some churches build schools and establish classes so that children and adults may be educated in their faith. Parishioners visit the sick in hospitals, nursing homes, and private homes to offer solace and spiritual encouragement to the aged and suffering. Church groups sponsor cleanup and building projects to enhance the living quarters of the urban and rural poor.

Besides direct help to the underprivileged, many Christians implementing the Social Gospel try to change the institutional structures that cause the injustice that others experience. In the early part of this century, leaders from Catholic and Protestant mainline denominations joined with labor leaders and workers to empower the exploited laborer. They worked to outlaw child labor, to provide for workmen's compensation, and to limit the laborers' working day to eight hours. Father John Ryan, a Catholic supporter of the Social Gospel, advocated a living wage for all workers, which led to the establishment of the federal minimum-wage laws.

Unjust treatment of Blacks in the South, especially lynching activity, became a focus of action for those trying to change this evil. Supported by white Social Gospel activists, Ida Wells (1862–1931), a Black journalist, founded an organization to counter the hanging of Blacks. Promotion of women's rights began in Protestant churches, which culminated in the Women's Suffrage Amendment in the early twentieth century. When young men and women left their homes to obtain work in the industrialized cities, safe housing became an issue. Protestants responded with YMCA and YWCA facilities, and Catholics founded Working Boys' and Working Girls' Homes.

As they engaged in these works of mercy and compassion for their neighbors, Christians were conscious of the teaching of Jesus, who told them to love their neighbors as themselves. Walter Raushenbusch (1868–1918) and Dorothy Day (1897–1980) combined the rescue or direct aid and empowerment aspects of the Social Gospel. Rauschenbusch was a Baptist minister who believed that Christians had a collective responsibility for the poor. His stance contradicted the American ideals of capitalism and individualism, which suggested that everyone should be able to care for himself/herself successfully. He viewed poverty as caused by human exploitation, not laziness, and as something that could be corrected by supporting political programs to change the laws that permitted the oppression. Individual capitalists were exploiting their workers, so he wrote extensively to raise the consciousness of Christians to the plight of the vulnerable in society.

Dorothy Day, with her friend Peter Maurin, cofounded a penny paper called the *Catholic Worker*. It was dedicated to principles of social justice and called for proper compensation, reasonable hours, and better conditions for workers. The paper's dedication to the cause of peace caused some controversy during World War II and the Korean and Vietnam wars. Dorothy Day remained true to her rejection of war, bloodshed, and violence in spite of the criticism aimed at her by her more military-minded contemporaries. She even spent time in jail as a witness to her beliefs of pacifism and nonviolence. She raised people's consciousness about the injustice of war and poverty through the newspaper and encouraged her followers to protest and demonstrate against violence and inequality. At the same time, her Catholic Worker homes provided shelter and food for the unfortunate and unemployed.

By combining the forces of direct aid or rescue techniques with the ability to influence legislation, Christians were able to make some progress toward the implementation of God's kingdom on this earth in America, which they still saw as the promised land of the New Covenant.

LIBERATION THEOLOGY

Liberation Theology emerged from Catholic theologians in Central and South America who wrote about the injustices and oppression of the poor by the wealthy elite. Some political and religious leaders perceived that the liberation theologians advocated the use of violence to gain the rights and dignity of the poor who lived in slums deprived of water, electricity, or sewage facilities. Because the liberationists used Marxist social analysis in uncovering the issues, the politically and economically powerful opposed the liberation theologians. Liberation theology stresses freedom from economic, racial, and cultural oppression and decries the sins of imperialism, colonialism, capitalism, and elitist governments that cause injustice. Liberation theologians cite the Old Testament prophet Amos, who warned the rich to treat the poor kindly and with justice. Observing Jesus' concern for the poor and powerless in society, the theologians advocate a preferential option for the poor by the Catholic Church.

Gustavo Guitierrez, a Peruvian theologian, wrote *A Theology of Liberation* in 1971 in which he encouraged the establishment of Christian base communities to become building blocks for a more just society. These small communities met periodically to discuss scripture, find mutual support, and plan for action. Sometimes priests and sisters met with the groups, but because of the clerical shortage the laity usually conducted the meetings. The large landowners, politicians, and some clergy from the hierarchy were fearful of the power of these base communities, which were growing into larger associations and networks. Some of the Roman Catholic bishops in Brazil approved of the Christian base communities, providing them with discussion guides and protecting them from hostile politicians. Basing their decision on the Vatican documents of social justice, many of the clergy defended the poor and oppressed against the laws that promoted violence against them. Many of the poor peasants were subject to torture, forced off the land, refused employment, and compelled to watch their children die of malnutrition and disease.

Military dictatorships began to attack the Catholic Church because of its alignment with the poor and the base communities. "Militaries martyred an estimated 800 bishops, priests, and nuns in Latin America during the 1970s and early 1980s" (Kee, 1998, p. 573). A movie was made about the dedication of Archbishop Romero to the poor and his subsequent assassination by the military while saying Mass in 1980. In the same year three American sisters and a laywoman were raped and murdered by security forces for their crime of assisting refugees with food and medicine. Six Jesuit missionaries and two laywomen were shot to death in 1989 for teaching principles of social justice at the University of Central America in San Salvador.

The fanatic persecution has decreased, but the base communities continue to meet to discuss their spiritual growth, to support one another, and to create a vibrancy in the Catholic Church led by the laity. The base community concept has reached much of North America where it is embedded in spiritual renewal movements often led by Catholic laity.

FEMININE THEOLOGY

Using the method of the liberation theologians, which mined the scriptures for statements upholding the poor and oppressed, feminine theologians found passages affirming women. They noticed how Jesus always treated women with dignity and respect, even though it was not a cultural pattern at that time. He upheld the poor widow instead of the rich Pharisee. He would not condemn the woman caught in adultery when her partner was nowhere to be found. Jesus had good friends and disciples among women with whom he associated freely. Yet many Christian churches do not treat women as equal to men.

Feminine theologians add the sin of sexism, which is promulgated by patriarchy, to the liberation theologians' list of social sins of colonialism, capitalism, communism, and imperialism. Women are kept in secondary positions by the more powerful men in patriarchal societies. Feminists refer to this situation as the sin of sexism because it is so embedded in the structures of society that it almost becomes acceptable. An example of an acceptable custom that some persons believe demeans women would be the wedding practice of the bride's father, who has had charge of her life, now handing over his responsibility to the groom.

Feminist scripture scholars and religious historians have worked together to uncover the history of women in the early church. Male writers of scripture, history, and theology have portrayed all of humanity as essentially male, so it is important for feminist scholars to uncover the contributions of women in each area.

Patriarchal interpretation of the gospels say that Jesus had only male apostles whom he ordained as priests at the Last Supper; therefore, Roman Catholic and Orthodox women cannot be ordained priests. Feminine biblical scholars point out that Jesus did not ordain anyone a priest because the Christian priesthood did not exist at that time. They also argue that women were numbered among the apostles, such as Junia, whom Paul calls an apostle in Romans 16. Mary Magdalene fits the definition of apostle, because she announced the resurrection of Christ and was sent by him to do so. Both male and female scripture scholars say that there is no evidence from scripture to bar women from the ordained priesthood. The Acts of the Apostles indicate that women led church services in their own house-churches. Similarly, there is evidence from the early tradition of the church that women participated fully in the liturgical life. Yet the hierarchy of Roman and Orthodox churches say that women cannot be priests because they cannot be icons of the male Christ. Christ in turn is an icon of God, which would indicate that God must be male. Feminists say that this maleness of God would present problems with the Bible's account of creation, "Let us make humans in our image, male and female they were created" (Gen. 1:27).

Roman and Orthodox Catholic churches have refused to ordain women as deacons. Religious historians have uncovered evidence that the order of deaconess, which began in the first century, continued in existence well into the fifth century. A list of clergy from the church of St. Sophia identified 80 male deacons and 40 female deaconesses in the fifth century. Many Protestant denominations have deaconesses assigned to liturgical functions, and some are ministers who lead their congregations. Some of the women ministers complain that they are assigned to the smaller congregations, serve as associate pastors, and are deprived from the larger decision-making boards. The Episcopalians have ordained women as priests and even as bishops. Feminist theologians say that the precedents have been made for women's full participation in their churches, but sexist traditions continue to discriminate against their gifts.

Pioneering feminine theologians have included both women and men in liturgical language. They have petitioned publishers of liturgical prayerbooks and hymns to use gender-inclusive terms in horizontal language that pertains to other people. For example, when Paul addresses only "brothers" in his letters, gender-inclusive language would say "brothers and sisters." Sarah's name would be included with Abraham in prayers mentioning their contributions as Christian ancestors. However, inclusive language has been sorely challenged by vertical language, or in words referring to God. Although God is a neutral word, the pronoun "he" is always used in sacred writings. Mary Daly (1973), a feminine theologian, claims that in the Judeo-Christian tradition, "God is male and the male is God" (p. 1). She says that this means that men are viewed as taking on the characteristics of God and women as possessing the lower characteristics of humans. Some feminists think that the use of male pronouns for God causes women to separate themselves from a God with whom they cannot identify. The Spirit is sometimes referred to as "she," but male-designated words for God seem to reinforce patriarchal concepts that denigrate women.

Feminine theologians see as their task to examine scripture, doctrines, practices, and institutions from a female perspective. Since women's experience differs from men's, they feel that it is imperative that women's voices be heard. Women, who tend to emphasize the relatedness of humans to each other, nature, and God, are sensitive to issues of equality, human dignity, and ecology.

SUMMARY

Christian concern for social and economic justice has sometimes met with opposition from those concerned with individualism, materialism, and consumerism. Christians' emphasis on community and the relatedness of all human beings causes their members to be concerned with human rights, equality and ecology. Following the words and example of Jesus, Christians extend themselves to the poor, homeless, and most vulnerable members of society. Catholics and mainline Protestants have been most vocal at advocating specific programs to alleviate the sufferings of the poor. They have spoken against the economic oppression of Third World members by capitalistic countries and have spoken for the cancellation of the huge debts owed by poor countries. Christians have raised the consciousness of governing bodies to the plight of refugees and other displaced people.

Loyal to their scriptures, Christians have spread the Social Gospel with efforts to help the needy directly and also to transform the structures in society that cause injustices. They realized that not all sins are personal but that social sins, such as racism, imperialism, colonialism, and discrimination against the underprivileged, reside in institutions. Efforts were made by socially conscious Christians to influence legislation regarding the plight of workers, treatment of Blacks, and women's suffrage.

Liberation theologians from Latin and South America encouraged the formation of small Christian base communities to discuss scripture and to empower the oppressed to action for a more just society. Military dictatorships saw the base communities as a threat to their established elitist position and began to persecute church leaders and members. The persecution has since decreased, and the Christian base communities continue to inspire and support their members in their efforts to preserve human dignity.

Feminine theologians added the sin of sexism caused by patriarchal societies and religions to the list of injustices directed at humans. Noting the generous example of Jesus toward women, they point out the discrepancy in treatment of women by institutional churches. They cite the role of women in the early church as a precedent for allowing women full participation in their contemporary churches. Feminine theologians have been more successful with inclusive language on the horizontal level than they been have been with inclusive language on the vertical level that pertains to God. However, they continue their efforts to raise the consciousness of the discrimination aimed at women by their Christian churches.

DISCUSSION QUESTIONS

1. Why do you think churches should be concerned with issues of social and economic justice?
2. Why is it important to consider at the same time both direct aid to the unfortunate and efforts to change the structures that cause injustice?
3. Is it a realistic expectation that humans can bring the kingdom of God to fulfillment on earth? Why or why not?
4. How is the Jubilee year connected to the cancellation of world debts?
5. Why would leaders in South and Central America fear the base communities as Marxist?
6. What are some of the goals of feminine theologians? Do you agree or disagree with them?

WORKS CITED

Daly, Mary. *Beyond God the Father: Towards a Philosophy of Women's Liberation.* Boston: Beacon Press, 1973.

Kee, Howard Clark, Emily Albu, Carter Lindberg, William J. Frost, and Dana Robert. *Christianity: A Social and Cultural History,* Second Edition. Upper Saddle River, NJ: Prentice Hall, 1998.

Oxfam International, "Poor Country Debt Relief?" *Quarterly Bulletin,* Fall, 1999.

Chapter Eleven

Diversity in Christianity

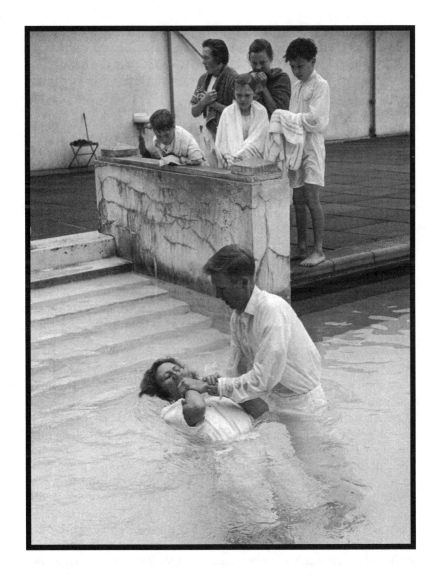

BENEFITS AND CHALLENGES OF PLURALISM

Pluralism, or the acceptance of a variety of religions, flourished in the United States, which had no established state religion. Pluralism exists because denominations recognize that there are common truths in a variety of churches and also because religious liberty as defined in the separation of church and state has legalized denominational equality. Christian America has a history of diversity starting with the Native Americans whose different tribes and nations had their own religions. The first immigrants from Europe brought their separate forms of Christianity with them. As the ethnic groups settled in America, they noticed that their neighbors differed from them in race, culture, national origin, and religion. Over time, neighbors realized that they must accept this pluralistic situation, from which they could derive many benefits and some challenges.

Pluralism inspires a variety of responses from Christians, some beneficial and others more challenging. The most obvious benefit is the ability to choose one's religious affiliation rather than be forced to belong to the established religion. Another benefit is that in the presence of a variety of religions, one is forced to reflect more consciously on one's own. Since each religion attributes truth to its beliefs and practices, its voluntary adherents must be cognizant of the scriptures, doctrines, rituals, and moral practices of its tradition. In a pluralistic society where one strives to accept other religions, one endeavors to understand the various beliefs and practices of those religious traditions. Pluralism can serve as an impetus not only for knowledge of one's own preferred religious tradition, but also for acquaintance with the religions of others. Knowledge enables differences to be respected rather than diminished or demeaned. Understanding, which is derived from knowledge, lessens hostility and suspicion toward the unknown. If one truly respects the pluralistic beliefs of a variety of religions, feverish activity to convert others (with its accompanying unpleasantness) is less likely to occur. Pluralism can be a most enriching experience where one can appreciate the various ways that God is worshipped and the methods by which individuals obtain meaning from life.

But pluralism can cause difficulties for Christians who believe that only their denomination holds absolute truth. They wonder if they can really be open to other religions without giving up loyalty to their own. They are concerned with the question, "How can all religions that differ from each other still hold the same truth?" Does truth differ for each religious group? Christians whose neighbors are Jews, Muslims, New Age advocates, or atheists may begin to wonder who has the real truth. These questions regarding the issue of truth can lead to a relativism that says that all religions hold some truth, so they must all be the same.

The questioner might decide to change denominations or forego religion entirely. Diversity of religion can also lead to a defensive posture in which the believers constantly attempt to reinforce their position of holding all truth. This exclusivist position claims that since there is only one truth, and it is contained in the believers' religious tradition, then it is the only right religion. The corollary to this stance is that all other religions must be wrong. This belief can lead to intense conversion activity, arrogance regarding statements concerning salvation, and labelling other groups as inferior or at least misguided.

Perhaps the most comforting thought regarding pluralism is that no religion need fear persecution. Pluralistic spiritualities have persuaded publishers to issue religious books from a variety of religious viewpoints. Some of the most popular TV shows, such as *Touched by an Angel* and *Promised Land* continue to attract a large number of viewers. Although Christian church attendance has appeared to decline recently, interest in religion and spirituality has increased. Some of this religious interest can be attributed to the variety of religious experiences that pluralism creates.

ATTEMPTS AT ECUMENISM

Some theologians, such as Wolfhart Pannenberg, have suggested that the twenty-first century will bring an end to multiple denominations and small religious groups. Only three divisions will remain: Catholic, Orthodox, and Evangelical. If that situation is to come about, some serious attempts at ecumenism must be made. Ecumenism is a movement toward the unity of all Christian churches. It began with attempts at cooperation between the churches in missionary, social, and educational endeavors. Some Christian churches shared seminaries, hospitals, and recreational facilities. Unity has been more difficult to attain in doctrinal and liturgical areas. Institutional authority presents a problem, but attempts at interdenominational dialogue have been promising in trying to overcome some of the obstacles to unity.

Protestant mainline denominations united to form the World Council of Churches, which held its first conference in Amsterdam in 1948. The WCC's efforts immediately following the war concentrated on service to refugees, loan funds, social and economic aid to underdeveloped nations, and appeals to governments to prohibit all weapons of mass destruction. Pope John XXIII attempted to improve relations between Catholics and other Christian groups. He emphasized the church's duty to work for "the full visible truth" among all Christians. Catholics and Protestants have met together to work on common efforts toward justice and peace and have achieved some goals that they could not effect alone. Some Orthodox groups have joined them, but the Fundamentalists and Evangelicals largely have not become involved in ecumenical efforts.

The National Council of Churches of Christ in America was formed in 1950 to achieve common goals of cooperation. Comprised of most mainline Protestant and some Orthodox churches, it was the successor to the Federal Council of Churches formed in 1908. The NCCCA affirms social action and justice activities but downplays doctrinal differences and attempts at evangelization. The magazine *Christian Century* reflects the liberal mainline Protestant viewpoints, while the *National Catholic Reporter* embodies the liberal Catholic perspective. Some Protestant denominations—such as the Presbyterians and Methodists, which separated from each other during the Civil War—have sought reunification. The Lutherans and Episcopalians are agreeing to share pulpits and communion. Presently, attempts at reunification are being made by other Protestant groups. Roman Catholics hope for a reunification with mainline Protestant denominations as voiced by recent popes.

ALTERNATIVE RELIGIONS

New religions arise periodically under a variety of circumstances. Freedom of religion allowed in the United States engenders their growth in this country, but other areas of the globe also have seen the emergence of new religions. Some groups can be called millennial, in that they expect the return of Christ as depicted in the Book of Revelation. Millennialist groups look forward to the Second Coming of Christ that will usher in a thousand (mille) years of happiness, bliss, and peace. Other groups look back to the idealized vision of the early church, which they perceive as the model to be imitated. They hold an exclusive attitude toward salvation that motivates them to ambitious evangelization and conversion efforts.

Mormons, or Church of Latter Day Saints

The Church of the Latter Day Saints was founded by Joseph Smith (1805–1844) in central New York State. He had a vision of the angel Moroni who presented him with two golden tablets, upon which was written the 531 pages of the Book of Mormon. The gold plates were returned to heaven, but Smith wrote down the information, which described the destination of a lost tribe of Israel to the United States in 600 B.C. Their descendants became the American Indians. The Mormons moved westward with Brigham Young to Salt Lake City, which became the world headquarters in 1847.

Although Mormons consider themselves Christian, other Christians question their beliefs because Mormons do not believe that the three persons of the Blessed Trinity are only one God. They also believe that God started out human and became divine, so humans who are created in God's image can become gods. Part of their creed says, "What man is now, God once was; what God is now, man can become" (Shipps, 1988, p. 659). Because it is necessary for souls who reside in heaven to become embodied, Mormons believe they should have as many children as possible. Polygamy as practiced by the men of the Old Testament was allowed in Utah until it became a state in 1896.

Mormons engage in ambitious proselytization, requiring their young people to dedicate a year of their lives to this effort. They believe that they are the one true religion and that America is the site of the New Jerusalem to be established in the millennium.

Seventh Day Adventists

Seventh Day Adventists held their first national conference in Michigan in 1863. Ellen White's (1827–1915) visions, in which she saw the words, "Keep Holy the Sabbath Day," helped to forge their beliefs. As a result, Seventh Day Adventists worship on the seventh day of the week, or Saturday. They are known for their healthy lifestyles of exercise and proper nutrition, including abstinence from caffeine, tobacco, and alcohol. Her followers, who consider Ellen White their prophetess, engage in much evangelization for their religion. Seventh

Day Adventists are present in America, Latin America, and Africa, preaching the need to ready oneself for the Second Coming (advent) of Christ.

Christian Scientists

Another religion in which a woman was instrumental is Christian Science, founded by Mary Baker Eddy (1821–1910). After a fall on an icy pavement, Eddy was confined to bed with severe injuries. One day, after reading about the healing miracles of Jesus, she felt herself instantly healed. She said that the healing ministry of Jesus did not end with the early church but continues through the power of the Spirit. People get sick because they rely on their own mortal minds. They will not be cured unless they tap into the divine mind of God. As a result, Christian Scientists do not accept the services of the medical profession but will go to hospitals only in acute cases. They are known for their Christian Science Reading Rooms, where students can find teachers and books for instruction. Their daily newspaper, *The Christian Science Monitor,* has received international recognition for its well-researched and well-written articles.

Jehovah's Witnesses

Organized by Charles Taze Russell (1852–1916), the Witnesses refer to God as Jehovah, a title used in the Old Testament. They believe that they witness to Jehovah and the imminent return of Christ by their door-to-door proselytization and distribution of their publication, *Watchtower.* They meet for Bible study in kingdom halls but have no clergy, because they are opposed to organized religion. They believe that only 144,000 people as depicted in the Book of Revelation will go to heaven, but after the millennium in Jehovah's reign, the rest of the Jehovah's Witnesses will live on the earth, which will be returned to its paradisal state. It will resemble the New Earth as depicted in the Book of Revelation.

Because they think that the present world is evil and that Satan controls it through his allies (the government, churches, and business), they refuse to salute the flag, serve in the armed forces, or celebrate Christian holidays. Witnesses do not accept blood transfusions because of the Old Testament prohibition against drinking blood. Their stance regarding transfusions has involved litigation with hospitals when children undergoing surgery, who cannot sign for themselves, are involved.

These millennial groups expect the imminent return of Christ to pass judgment on the people of the earth. Some persons outside their groups will be condemned, but because of their loyalty to their faith community, their members will be saved. Millennial groups have a strong sense of belonging to a community of faith that shares their values and goals. They receive security from their knowledge that they will be saved, which can be very reassuring to people who live in an atmosphere of questioning and ambiguity in American culture.

LATE TWENTIETH-CENTURY RELIGIOUS CULTS

Religious cults are usually biblically based and led by a strong, paternal authority figure who sees the group as being in constant struggle against a world perceived as evil. By following the words of the leader, the group will be assured of salvation and victory over the battle against evil. The group is totally committed to the leader and to each other, as well as to their leader's interpretation of scripture. Many of the cult members live communally and turn all their money over to the leader. They usually leave their families and friends, whom the cult members label as deceived because they reside in the evil world. Some of the cults, such as the Unification Church and the Boston Church of Christ, do much of their proselytizing on college campuses, appealing to lonely and confused students undergoing the strain of transition.

Unification Church

The followers of the Unification Church are often called Moonies after their founder, Sun Myung Moon (b.1920). He is considered by his followers to be the real messiah and the perfect parent, because although Jesus accomplished a spiritual redemption, he did not accomplish a full redemption because he had no children. Only Moon, a full parent, could model the perfect family to which his followers aspire, so he must be the true messiah. Reverend Moon and his wife choose the marriage partners for his followers and preside over the ceremonies that unite them. The young members live a very restrictive life of prayer, fund raising, and proselytizing, working long days and nights. They achieve a sense of satisfaction and purpose, believing that by transforming their own families into more perfect ones, they will transform society and then the world.

Boston Church of Christ

Members of the Boston Church of Christ do not live in communes but meet in rented halls where they enthusiastically respond to Bible readings with singing and clapping. Each member has a discipler, or mentor, in whom he or she must confide; members are requested to leave all their friends and family who are not members of the church. They are expected to give money to the church and to use their energy in proselytizing efforts. Conversion efforts are aimed especially at college students and young adults.

Branch Davidians

Followers of David Koresh (1959–1993) lived a communal life in Waco, Texas. They expected to establish a triumphant Davidic kingdom, similar to King David's kingdom, where the chosen 144,000 persons from the Book of Revelation would live in happiness and peace. First, a final apocalyptic battle would occur between good and evil, which Koresh described in terms of Seven Seals from the Book of Revelation. The U.S. Government was labelled by Koresh as an evil enemy with whom the Branch Davidians would engage in the battle. He saw himself as the final manifestation of Christ's spirit on earth and claimed to have direct revelation from God. Koresh demanded that the young male members abstain from sex with their wives. He alone would impregnate the women so that the children of the commune would be descendants of the prophet (himself). The government feared that the large cache of weapons in the compound would be used against them and that sexual abuse of children was occurring. Most of the community was killed when the commune was engulfed in flames as federal law enforcement agents invaded it.

SUMMARY

Religious pluralism presents benefits and challenges. Most Americans would not want to return to the established religions of Europe and Asia because they enjoy the freedom to choose their own religious affiliation. Pluralistic religions inspire the desire for more knowledge of one's own and other religions. The issue of truth can present a challenge in that it can lead to relativism or an intense conversion activity on the part of the "saved."

Ecumenical activity has fostered cooperation between various Christian denominations, especially in the areas of missionary, social, and educational endeavors. Protestant mainline denominations united to form the World Council of Churches to accomplish humanitarian goals they could not do alone. Catholics have cooperated on ecumenical talks and actions to address world problems. Members of the National Council of Churches of America and various smaller groups, including Catholics, engage in social action and peace activities.

Freedom of Religion in America has given impetus to the birth of new religions with connections to the Christian Bible. Some are millennial groups, such as the Mormons and the Seventh Day Adventists. The Christian Scientists and Jehovah Witnesses do not refer as much to the Second Coming of Christ as to the power of God to accomplish the perfect kingdom of the future.

Biblically based cults have arisen, led by powerful paternal figures such as Sun Myung Moon and David Koresh. They appeal to their adherents' need for security by promising safety and surety against an evil outside world. Cults build a strong sense of belonging and relieve their members from questioning issues or beliefs of the ambiguous society from which they fled.

DISCUSSION QUESTIONS

1. What are some of the advantages and disadvantages of pluralism? Do you think the advantages outweigh the disadvantages? Why or why not?
2. Why do you think that mainline Catholic and Protestant denominations are more likely than Evangelicals and Fundamentalists to engage in ecumenical activity?
3. Do you think that ecumenical activity might lead to the merging of some Protestant denominations? What evidence do we have of some merging occurring in the present?
4. Why do you think that alternative religions have arisen in America? What is their connection to millennialism?
5. What is the attraction of cults? What would you advise someone who is about to join a cult?

WORKS CITED

Mattingly, Terry. "Conservative Ecumenism." Scripps and Howard News Service, August 16, 1995.

Shipps, Jan. "The Latter Day Saints," in Charles Lippy and Peter Williams (eds.), *Encyclopedia of the American Religious Experience*. New York: Scribners, 1988, p. 659.

Appendix A:
Important Christian Dates

2000 B.C.	Abraham and the Covenant with God
1200 B.C.	Moses and the Ten Commandments
1000 B.C.	Kings David and Solomon and the Temple
400 B.C.	The Torah or First Five Books of the Bible Accepted
63 B.C.	Romans Capture and Dominate Palestine
c.0–4 B.C.	Jesus born in Palestine
A.D. 29–33	Preaching and Death of Jesus
A.D. 50–60	Paul's Writing of the Epistles
A.D. 65	Death of Peter and Paul
A.D. 70–95	Gospels are Written
A.D. 65–303	Persecutions of the Christians
A.D. 313	Constantine Issues Edict of Milan
A.D. 325	Council of Nicea, Addressing the Divinity of Christ
A.D. 367	Letter of Athanasius, Determining Canon of Scripture
A.D. 451	Council of Chalcedon, Dealing with Humanity of Christ
A.D. 525	Benedict and Monasticism in the West
A.D. 1054	Division of Western and Eastern Catholicism
A.D. 1100–1700	Building of the Great Cathedrals
A.D. 1450	Invention of the Printing Press
A.D. 1517	Protestant Reformation Begins
A.D. 1545	Council of Trent to Reform the Catholic Church
A.D. 1607	First Anglican Church in Jamestown, Virginia
A.D. 1636	Roger Williams and Beginning of Religious Toleration
A.D. 1787	Constitution Defines Religious Freedom
A.D. 1948	World Council of Churches Established
A.D. 1962–65	Second Vatican Council to Modernize Catholicism

Appendix B:
Relevant Web Sites

http://www.iclnet.org/pub/resources/christian-resources.html

http://www.yahoo.com/Society_and_Culture/Religion_and_Spirituality/Faiths_and_Practices/Christianity

http://www.cs.cmu.edu/Web/People/spok/catholic/teaching.html

http://www.christusrex.org/

http:sunsite.unc.edu./expo.vatican.exhibit/Vatican exhibit.html

http://www.webdesk.com/catholic/prayers/index.html

http://www.teleport.com/~arden/religium.htm

http://dir.lycos.com/Society/Religion_and_Spirituality/Faiths_and_Beliefs/Christianity

http://www.csis.org.uk

http://directory.netscape.com/Society/Religion_and_Spirituality/Faiths_and_Beliefs/Christianity

http://cultawarenessnetwork.org

Index